Tim Kers...

Colour illustra...
Krzysztof W. W...

Gloster
Grebe and
Gamecock

STRATUS

Published in Poland in 2011
by STRATUS s.c.
Po. Box 123,
27-600 Sandomierz 1, Poland
e-mail: office@mmpbooks.biz
for
Mushroom Model Publications,
3 Gloucester Close, Petersfield,
Hampshire GU32 3AX, UK.
e-mail: rogerw@mmpbooks.biz
© 2011 Mushroom Model
Publications.
http://www.mmpbooks.biz

ISBN
978-83-61421-17-7

Editor in chief
Roger Wallsgrove

Editorial Team
Bartłomiej Belcarz
Artur Juszczak
James Kightly
Robert Pęczkowski

DTP
Robert Pęczkowski
Krzysztof W. Wołowski

Colour Drawings
Krzysztof W. Wołowski

Scale Plans
Krzysztof W. Wołowski

Printed by:
Drukarnia Diecezjalna,
ul. Żeromskiego 4,
27-600 Sandomierz
tel. (15) 832 31 92;
fax (15) 832 77 87
www.wds.pl marketing@wds.pl

PRINTED IN POLAND

Dedication

In fond memory of Roff T Jones 1919-2006
Design team leader

and of Barry Denton 1927- 2004
Construction team leader

And to all other members of the Jet Age Museum Gamecock team,
past and present.

Książka poświęcona pamięci Krzysztofa.
In memory of Krzysztof.

Krzysztof W. Wołowski
19.06.1961- 04.03.2011

Acknowledgements

This book would not have been possible without the archives of Gloucestershire Aviation Collection's Jet Age Museum. I am grateful to the museum's
chairman and trustees for making them available. I have also had invaluable
help from aviation historians Phil Butler and Tony Buttler. Thanks also to
Erika Oughton for the loan of her late husband Jim Oughton's superb collection and to Rex Meaden for allowing the use of his late father Jack Meaden's
unfinished, unpublished typescript The Gloster Story, which has made a
major contribution to the text. Finally, thanks to publisher Roger Wallsgrove
of Mushroom Model Publications for his generous and enthusiastic support.

Photographs are credited wherever possible, but in many cases the sources
are unknown. Any further information would be welcome.

Table of contents

Introduction

Grebe and Gamecock: two of the names most evocative of the Royal Air Force in the 1920s. The radial-engined Grebe of 1923, dainty and nimble, was the first new fighter design to enter RAF service after the end of the First World War, replacing the old rotary-engined Sopwith Snipes. It was also the first of a distinguished line of Gloster fighters to serve with the RAF.

Its successor, the Gamecock, beefier but just as agile, was the RAF's last wire-braced wooden fighter. Both Grebe and Gamecock were superb aerobatic machines, thrilling the crowds at the annual RAF Display at Hendon. Neither saw active service, although the Gamecock came close in the Finnish-Russian Winter War and one served with the Finnish Air Force until 1944.

In the 1926 RAF Display at Hendon two Wings of three squadrons of nine aircraft took part, a total of 54 service fighters. Of these, no less than 45 were Grebes or Gamecocks (the other nine were Siskins).

To begin with they were known as the Gloucestershire Grebe and Gamecock, the products of the Gloucestershire Aircraft Company (GAC) of Sunningend, Cheltenham. They are better known as the Gloster Grebe and Gamecock, from the name the company adopted on 11 November 1926 - the simplified name was easier for foreign customers to spell and pronounce.

Above: Henry Folland's first accredited design, the Royal Aircraft Factory SE4 of 1914, was criticised for being "too fast". (Walwin Collection)
Below: Royal Aircraft Factory chief test pilot Frank Goodden in the cockpit of the first SE5. Goodden died when it broke up in the air, but the type was developed into one of the finest fighters of the First World War. (Walwin Collection)

Both aircraft were designed by the great Henry Folland and his inseparable assistant Henry Preston. They already had a reputation for single-seat fighter design before they started work with GAC in 1921. Both had been in the design office of the Royal Aircraft Factory at Farnborough under Geoffrey de Havilland. Folland had designed the startlingly fast SE4 of 1914 and went on to be lead designer of the SE5 and its famous successor the SE5a, one of the outstanding British fighters of the First World War.

When the Factory's design team was dispersed in 1916 Folland and Preston joined "British Nieuport", as the Nieuport and General Aircraft Company was known. The Cricklewood-based firm was entirely British, owned by Sir Samuel (later Lord) Waring, and had been set up originally as Nieuport (England) to produce French Nieuport company designs under licence. Folland became its first in-house designer and designed the BN1, Nighthawk and Nightjar fighters, the London bomber and the Nieuhawk and Goshawk racers, all of them British aircraft in spite of their Nieuport name.

Folland left Farnborough for Nieuport & General in 1917 and designed the BN1 as a successor to his SE5. (Walwin Collection)

Folland's BN1, intended as a Camel replacement, was powered by a Bentley BR2 rotary engine and designed to use as many SE5a components as possible - the thread which links Folland's designs can be followed through to the Grebe, the Gamecock and beyond. The BN1 flew in February 1918 and competed at Martlesham with the Sopwith Snipe. It was 17 mph (27 km/h) faster at 15,000 feet (4572 m) and had an absolute ceiling 4,500 feet (1372 m) greater, but it was destroyed by fire in mid-air on 10 March. The Snipe won the competition (other competitors were the Austin Osprey and the Boulton and Paul Bobolink) and went on to enter service with the Royal Flying Corps. In due course it became the RAF's first standard peacetime fighter until the arrival of Gloster's Grebe and the Armstrong-Whitworth Siskin.

After the disappointment of the BN1, Folland undertook a fundamental redesign. The new Nighthawk fighter was powered by the ABC Dragonfly, a radial engine of great promise. The Dragonfly was ordered in vast numbers (more than 11,000) to power many of the RAF's next generation of fighters and bombers. If the First World War had continued into 1919 it would have been catastrophic for the British war in the air: the Dragonfly was spectacularly underpowered and unreliable.

Folland's Nighthawk, however, became the true forerunner of the Grebe and Gamecock. It was a two-bay biplane designed to the new Air Board's first specification, Type A1(a) of April 1917. It incorporated as many components as possible from the SE5a, most obviously its underfin and tailskid, and the empennage of the BN1: a sharply-sloping fin, distinctive curved rudder and a tailplane with a large-radius curve to its leading edge.

The Nighthawk was an excellent machine, in spite of its Dragonfly engine. Oliver Stewart wrote that *"aerobatic pilots found a machine which might have been made expressly for their benefit. ... It was capable of great rapidity of manoeuvre and it possessed extraordinarily well-balanced controls. ... It was a delight to handle"*.

British Nieuport received orders for 150 Nighthawks, subcontracting part of the order to the newly-formed Gloucestershire Aircraft Company. This had been set up in June 1917 as a joint venture of the Aircraft Manufacturing Co (Airco) and the distinguished

The first Nighthawk in Nieuport & General's Cricklewood factory. Folland designed the Nighthawk after the loss of the BN1. It would have been one of the new RAF's front line fighters if the war had continued into 1919. (Walwin Collection)

The first civil Nighthawk, K151, was registered on 13 June 1919 and entered in the Aerial Derby a week later. Converted into a two-seater, it was re-registered G-EAEQ when the first permanent UK register was adopted the following month. (Author's collection)

Cheltenham-based architectural crafts company HH Martyn, which had already done a great deal of top-quality sub-contract work for Airco.

Exact Nighthawk production is not certain. It is believed that, apart from the three prototypes, a further 70 were built, with another 54 as engine-less airframes. The order was cancelled and the Nighthawk never saw war service, but several were used for a variety of tests at Farnborough, Martlesham and the Isle of Grain. Some were retained by British Nieuport and in single and two-seat versions they were raced after the war under the names Nighthawk and Nieuhawk. A heavily-modified Nighthawk with circular cross-section fuselage and

Folland's Dragonfly-engined Nieuport Goshawk racer was a heavily-modified Nighthawk with cut-down wings, single I interplane struts and fuselage faired to circular section. It competed in the 1920 Aerial Derby. Harry Hawker, the famous Sopwith test pilot, lost his life in this aircraft. (Walwin Collection)

drastically reduced wingspan saw some racing success as the Goshawk, a striking sight in blue and yellow chequers overall. It was destroyed after Harry Hawker, Sopwith's famous test pilot, suffered a haemorrhage during a practice flight for the 1921 Aerial Derby.

Following the Armistice of 11 November 1918, orders from the Air Ministry - the Air Board's successor - dried up. The market was swamped with surplus aircraft and aero engines at knockdown prices and the British aircraft industry went into near-terminal decline. The Snipe and the Bristol Fighter, both available in large numbers, were chosen as standard equipment for the peacetime RAF. By 1922 there was only one fighter squadron based in Britain, 25 Squadron, equipped with Snipes.

Gloucestershire Aircraft Company was determined to stay in business. Director David Longden, supported by fellow directors AW Martyn, Hugh Burroughes and Guy Peck, realised that orders must start flowing again at some stage, but GAC had no design staff. The directors engaged Henry Folland as a consultant, with the job of putting GAC on the map and winning official orders. In the space of six weeks GAC's first in-house design was designed, built and test flown. It was a hotrod racer powered by a Napier Lion water-cooled in-line engine. The rear fuselage and tail were surplus Nighthawk, the wings essentially Goshawk. The upper wing was supported on a distinctive "hump" containing the main fuel tank. The authorised designation was Mars I but when a resourceful reporter from a London daily managed to see the uncovered aircraft before completion and asked what it would be called, Folland came up with the name Bamel on the spur of the moment, according to GAC's inspector Christopher Woodgate, saying "*She somewhat resembles a camel, also the rear half is bare*". The Bamel soon won the 1921 Aerial Derby and set a British air speed record.

GAC and Folland capitalised on the Bamel's celebrity by buying up surplus Nighthawk airframes from the Air Ministry. The Dragonfly engine was completely discredited by now, so Folland redesigned the Nighthawk to take the tried-and-tested, reliable and easily available Bentley BR2 rotary. In this form, known as the Sparrowhawk, it was ordered in quantity in 1921 by the Imperial Japanese Navy's fledgling air arm. The Sparrowhawk I (also known as the Mars II) was a land-based single-seat fighter, the Sparrowhawk II (Mars III) a two-seat trainer and the Sparrowhawk III (Mars IV) a single-seat shipborne fighter. Fifty of them, all Nighthawks reconditioned and modified by GAC in Cheltenham, were sold to Japan, together with spares and components for another 40 machines.

When British Nieuport went into liquidation in 1922, Folland was engaged full-time by GAC, becoming chief engineer and designer. The Bamel was the perfect advertisement for the company, a high-performance machine from a respected designer, and it went on to win the Aerial Derby again in 1922 and (as the Gloster I) in 1923.

The part played by Folland's racing machines in the development of the Grebe was recognised by Flight magazine. In its issue of 29 October 1925 it stated: "*The Gloucestershire Aircraft Co has ever since its formation pursued a very strong racing policy. ... That the firm's belief in the useful purpose served by air racing was justified is proved by the success of the Gloster 'Grebe' with its developments now being supplied to the Royal Air Force, which is a direct outcome of the firm's experience with racing machines.*"

In addition to the Japanese order, one more Sparrowhawk was built, a two-seater Sparrowhawk II. It was retained by the company, registered as G-EAYN, and used as a demonstrator. Leslie Tait-Cox flew it in the 1922 Aerial Derby but failed to finish. The airframe became the basis for the Grebe's immediate predecessor, the Gloucestershire Grouse.

After fulfilling the Japanese Navy order Gloster retained one Sparrowhawk II and registered it as G-EAYN. It was raced at Croydon on 17 September 1921. Heavily modified, it would later be transformed into the Grouse, the first of Gloster's HLB biplanes. (Via JD Oughton)

Grouse

The Gloucestershire Grouse was an experimental aircraft, the first to test the patented High Lift Biplane (HLB) configuration. Patent No. 225,257 was applied for on 26 July 1923 by "*The Gloucestershire Aircraft Company, ... Henry Phillip Folland FRAeS MBE MIAeE and Henry Edward Preston*". The application states that "*the main object of our invention is to provide biplane wings of increased efficiency whereby the weight and dimensions thereof can be reduced and the stability and controllability of the aircraft improved*". The configuration had, in fact, already been incorporated in "*a Gloucestershire Goods Type Commercial Aeroplane*" for which Folland completed the design the previous year, although it was not built.

The new wings were fitted to G-EAYN and thus the Sparrowhawk became the Grouse. A larger, thicker-section upper wing provided maximum lift and was paired with a smaller, thinner section lower wing. The latter was also set at a lower angle of incidence: it provided maximum lift for take-off and landing combined with minimum drag at speed. Another novel feature was the absence of an upper wing centre section, the two wings meeting on the centre line and being supported by inverted vee cabane struts. The distinctive Nighthawk tailplane was retained but the Grouse was given the SE5A's fin and rudder. The forward cockpit was faired over.

The two main fuel tanks were fitted in the upper wings, projecting noticeably below the lower surface, a feature of all the subsequent Grebe-Gamecock series. The upper wing ailerons were reverse-tapered, with much greater chord at the tips than at the inner end.

It went to Martlesham on 11 May 1923 and was flown extensively during the summer. The HLB wings proved to be an effective combination. In spite of a reduction of 65 sq ft (6 sq m) in wing area, the stalling speed was reduced to 47 mph (76 km/h), 4 mph (6.4 km/h) lower than the same aircraft with its original Nighthawk wings. Its maximum speed was slightly increased and at 128 mph (206 km/h) was now 8 mph (13 km/h) faster than the top speed of the Bentley-engined Snipe fighter. According to Tim Mason, "*Results were sufficiently impressive for a version, named the Grebe, to be ordered for service use.*"

When the Grouse returned from Martlesham the company changed the Bentley for the new seven-cylinder Armstrong Siddeley Lynx radial engine of 185 hp (138 kW), the smaller brother of the 14-cylinder Jaguar which would power the new Grebe. The two-seat configuration was reinstated and the wingspan increased. Later an oleo undercarriage was fitted and the ailerons were enlarged. Gloster hoped that the Grouse II, as it was now known, would win RAF orders as a training machine. Gloster inspector Basil Fielding wrote: "*It was a very pleasant aircraft to fly in*".

RAF orders were not forthcoming but the Grouse II was fitted with Folland and Preston's

The Gloucestershire Grouse in its original configuration with Bentley BR2 engine, built to test Folland and Preston's HLB wing combination. A rebuild of Gloucestershire Sparrowhawk II G-EAYN, itself a modified Nieuport Nighthawk, its other new features include fuel tanks mounted on the upper wing, a faired-over front cockpit and SE5a-style vertical tail surfaces. Best guess for the colour scheme is gloss white and red, assessed by comparing the tone of the dark paint with the red and blue on a company photograph of the Grebe prototype known to have been taken afterwards. (Author's collection)

oleo undercarriage and sold to the Swedish Army Aviation Company as an advanced trainer. It was delivered shortly before the formation of the Swedish Air Force in the summer of 1926. Still registered as G-EAYN on delivery, it was allotted Swedish Air Force number 62 and given the designation Ö3. Based at Wing F3 at Malmen, it was finally written off in 1929 after 109 hours flying. Although the pilots were said to be impressed by the good performance of the Grouse, no more orders followed.

Grouse details

Gloucestershire Sparrowhawk II development to test patented HLB wing configuration used on Grebe and Gamecock. Single or two-seat experimental aircraft, later trainer. One built: British civil registration G-EAYN, later Swedish military serial 62.

Construction:
Wire-braced wooden structure, fabric covered.

Engine:
Mk I: 230 hp (172 kW) Bentley BR2 rotary. Mk II: 185 hp (138 kW) Armstrong-Siddeley Lynx radial.

Dimensions:
Mk I: Span 27 ft (8.23 m). Length 19 ft (5.79 m). Height 10 ft 1 in (3.07 m). Wing area 205 sq ft (19.04 sq m). Mk II: Span increased to 27 ft 10 in (8.48 m). Length increased to 20 ft 4 in (6.2 m). Height reduced to 9 ft 5 in (2.87 m). Wing area reportedly unchanged at 205 sq ft (19.04 sq m).

Performance and weights:
Mk I: top speed 128 mph (206 km/h) at sea level. Climb to 10,000 ft (3048 m) 11 min. Service ceiling 19,000 ft (5791 m). All-up weight 2,120 lb (961.6 kg). Tare weight 1,375 lb (623.7 kg).
Mk II: top speed 120 mph (193 km/h) at sea level. Climb to 10,000 ft (3048 m) 17 min. Service ceiling 18,000 ft (5486 m). All-up weight 2,118 lb (960.7 kg). Tare weight 365 lb (165.6 kg).

Another view of the Bentley-engined Grouse, clearly showing the faired-over front cockpit and the SE5-style fin and rudder. (Via JD Oughton)

Reinstated as a two-seater, the Grouse in its Mark II form was fitted with a seven-cylinder Armstrong Siddeley Lynx engine and the fuselage was slimmed down. The rear cabane struts were mounted further forward to allow entry to the cockpit and an additional pair of cabane stuts were fitted at the front. Colour scheme is not known. The occupants are the company's HE Austin in the front cockpit and inspector Basil Fielding in the rear. (Via Jet Age Museum)

Further modified for Sweden and numbered 62, the Lynx-engined Grouse had an oleo undercarriage, parallel-chord ailerons, revised windscreens and no tailskid fairing, a far cry from its original Sparrowhawk II identity. The photograph has been crudely retouched, with the pilot painted in. (Via Jet Age Museum)

Grebe

Prototypes and testing

The Grebe was a landmark design. Aviation historian John WR Taylor wrote: "*For years these little biplanes thrilled crowds at air displays all over the country, but, more than that, they marked a great step forward in the evolution of British fighter aircraft and experimental work carried out with Grebes bore a marked influence on later designs*".

The first three Grebes were built by GAC to Air Ministry Specification 3/23 (File no 406052/23). Their serials were J6969, J6970 and J6971 and they were built under Contract no 402023/23 issued on 21 February 1923. At this stage the name Grebe had not been given to the new type and its ancestry was recognised in the specification, which referred to the aircraft as "Nighthawk with Thick Wing Section".

All the prototypes were powered by Armstrong-Siddeley's 350 hp Jaguar III 14-cylinder radial engine. They had conventional V-strut undercarriages at this stage. The Grebe's ancestry was apparent in the SE5a-style fin, rudder, underfin and tailskid, while the tailplane and elevators were the same as on the Nighthawk. Indeed, Harald Penrose wrote of the Grebe's public debut at Hendon that the "*new and pretty single-seat Gloucestershire Grebe ... was obviously a re-designed, modernised and streamlined SE5*". Construction was standard for the time: a wire-braced, fabric-covered wooden structure of ash and spruce with metal fittings. Quoting Penrose again: "*design details ... remained almost unchanged from the Nieuport Nighthawk*".

The first Grebe, J6969, first flew in May 1923, piloted by Gloucestershire's test pilot Larry Carter. It went to Martlesham on 22 June for service trials and made its public debut at the Hendon RAF Pageant just over a week later, on 30 June, wearing a prominent number 14. Martlesham's report, number 343 of July 1923, recorded a maximum speed of 147 mph (237 km/h) at 6,500 feet (1981 m). It climbed to 15,000 feet (4572 m) in just under 15 minutes, had a service ceiling of 20,950 feet (6386 m) and endurance of 3 1/2 hours. One pilot reported that it handled "delightfully". J6969 then went to the Royal Aircraft Establishment (RAE) at

The first Grebe prototype, J6969, at Brockworth, clearly showing its SE5 ancestry in the fin, rudder and tailskid. It first flew in May 1923. (Via JD Oughton)

Grebe prototype (probably J6969) at Brockworth airfield. Note early-style undercarriage, fuel tanks and ailerons. (Via Jet Age Museum)

Farnborough on 24 July , where it was used for instrument tests and later for heated clothing trials. After a short spell back at Gloster beginning in March 1924, it returned to the RAE on 16 April for general and high altitude tests. Its last flight was on 24 August 1925.

J6970, the second prototype Grebe, went to Martlesham on July 1923 and remained there for about a year and a half. It underwent consumption tests and was later subjected to comparative testing with the Armstrong-Siddeley Siskin for manoeuvrability and general handling. Its rate of climb was a little greater than the first Grebe and its service ceiling a little higher. High oil temperatures were reported, indicating inadequate cooling, and a modified Jaguar was installed in June 1924. In March 1925 it was taken back to Gloster for major repairs, eventually returning to Martlesham, where it stayed from February 1926 until April 1927.

Grebe prototype J6969 at Hendon, numbered "14" for the RAF Display on 30 June 1923. (Author's collection)

All that has been recorded of the third prototype, J6971, is that after a spell with Gloster it then went to Martlesham, returning to Gloster in August 1924.

A prototype was also built by the company for its own use and registered as G-EBHA on 29 June 1923. It first flew on 6 July

1923 piloted by Larry Carter and its Certificate of Airworthiness was issued on 11 July. Also in July it took part in the King's Cup Air Race as the scratch machine, entered by Sir William Joynson-Hicks and piloted by Larry Carter. It was in second place on the outward leg but suffered a broken landing wire soon after leaving Glasgow and had to retire. Nonetheless, Carter received the Manchester Guardian prize of £25 for the fastest time between Glasgow and Manchester.

Soon afterwards it was flown from Rotterdam to Gothenburg, a distance of 700 miles, and won the Swedish prize for the fastest speed. It went on to be used as a company demonstrator and as an experimental machine. The Certificate of Airworthiness expired on 29 July 1929. It was withdrawn from use and scrapped in 1930.

Into production

It was clear to GAC that a production order would follow, although the company was disappointed in its hope that it would receive a parallel order for the Grouse as a two-seat trainer. Recruiting workers was a priority. Former Gloster chief inspector Basil Fielding wrote: "*During the 1914-18 war, I am told 300 men were employed in the Sheet Metal Department, but afterwards owing to lack of work it dwindled down to five. When the contract for Grebes was received ... many of the old hands were taken on again*". H Hall, then living in Fulham, received a letter from GAC dated 9 July 1923: "*We are now in a position to offer you employment as a Sheet Metal Worker, and shall be glad if you will take up work here at the earliest possible moment.*" The wages offered were "*1/9d per hour Flat Rate until August 1st, after that date 1/8d per hour, plus Piece Work Earnings.*"

After the trials the Grebe design was modified and went into production for the Royal Air Force as the Grebe II, the prototypes being retrospectively designated Grebe I. A total of 109 Grebe II fighters were built. In 1925 another 20 dual-control Grebes would be ordered, designated Grebe IIIDC. A handful of single-seaters would also be converted to dual control.

Frank McKenna FRAeS, who was works manager at the time, wrote in 1955 that the initial order for Grebes was "*the biggest order placed in the industry for single-seat fighters since the Armistice in 1918. But the firm was not allowed to bask in the sunshine of such prosperity... There was a request by the Ministry to the effect that since [Gloster] had managed by their successful design to corner the single-seat fighter market, they must sub-contract wings and tail units to Hawker, de Havilland and AV Roe to keep them going. Accordingly the 66 sets of top wings plus spares were placed with AV Roe and Company, the bottom wings with Hawker and the tail units and ailerons with de Havilland. The manufacture and assembly of the remainder of the aircraft was all [Gloster's] own!*"

The first production Grebe - the first Grebe II - was J7283. A company photograph of the new machine is captioned "Grebe (Service Type)". The most obvious difference from the Grebe I is that it is fitted with two Vickers guns on top of the forward fuselage, World War I style. It also has a new design of oleo undercarriage employing rubber shock absorbers in a streamlined casing, the subject of British Patent no 223,661 applied for on 26 July 1923

The second Grebe prototype, J6970, spent most of its time at Martlesham. It went there in July 1923, came back to Gloster in March 1925 and returned to Martlesham for another 14 months from February 1926. (Via Phil Butler)

The brand new first Grebe Mk II J7283 poses at Brockworth with machine guns fitted. It first flew in August 1923. (Jet Age Museum/Russell Adams Collection)

- the same date as the HLB wing patent application - by the Gloucestershire Aircraft Company, Folland and Preston. They stated: "*The object is to provide a shock absorber which shall be of such a shape that its resistance to the air is reduced to a minimum whilst its shock absorbing quality may be as great as possible and which may be of simple and cheap construction*". This was achieved by alternating rubber pads and metal plates around a main undercarriage oleo.

The two petrol tanks in the upper wings were redesigned and simplified, now rectangular in plan and with a shallow convex underside. On some Grebes the open exhausts of the prototype's Jaguar engine were later replaced by a collector ring to the rear of the engine and twin exhaust pipes running under the lower wing, ending behind the cockpit.

J7283 was the first of 12 Grebe II aircraft ordered on Contract no 468248/23 of March 1924, all to be fitted with the improved Jaguar IV engine of 400 hp (298 kW). It first flew in August 1923 with the Jaguar III engine and went to Martlesham in October, where it underwent extensive performance trials between then and July 1924.

J7283 at Gloster's Sunningend Works in Cheltenham. It carried the number "1" for the 1924 RAF Display, held at Hendon on 28 June. (Via Jet Age Museum)

Six Grebes from the first production batch lined up with Folland's tiny Gloucestershire Gannet light aircraft on Brockworth airfield. They include J7291, J7292 and J7293. None have guns fitted. The seventh Grebe, extreme left, is the company's own G-EBHA with early-style undercarriage and fuel tanks. (Via Jet Age Museum)

The previous month, on 28 June, it was at the annual Hendon RAF Display bearing the large number 1 on each side of the fuselage ahead of the roundel.

Martlesham reported favourably on the new oleo undercarriage but also encountered for the first time the Grebe's tendency to serious wing flutter. Jack Meaden records that Hubert Broad, the famous test pilot, was flying a Grebe at full throttle on 15 September 1924. It developed aileron flutter which caused high speed vibration of the control column. The vibration stopped again when Broad closed the throttle, but was later found to have split the main spars.

Several sources refer to the unreliability of the Grebe's Jaguar engine, but Basil Fielding wrote: "*The engine gave very little trouble but care had to be taken in setting up the tappet clearances which were very large, these closed in when the engine got warmed up. There was no compensation gear to allow for this as there was on the later type Bristol engines. A bad snag I remember was the screwed cap on the carburettor. The threads picked up and many caps had to be drilled out. This was remedied on later types by using a different material*".

Some sources state that the first batch of production Grebes were ordered to Specification number 37/23, but Meekcoms and Morgan make it clear that this specification was for the Jupiter-engined development of the Grebe, which became the Gamecock.

Grebes in squadron service

In September 1924 J7283 went to both 56 and 25 Squadron for service trials before returning to Martlesham. In the same month Grebes allegedly entered squadron service proper. Grebe squadrons are described below in the order in which they first received their new aircraft.

111 Squadron

There's some confusion here. 111 Squadron, newly reformed at Duxford as part of the Air Defence of Great Britain, is said to have operated a single Flight of Grebes from as early as October 1923 through to June 1924, according to Rawlings, or until January 1925, according to Jefford, who records that they were joined by the Sopwith Snipe from April 1924 and the Armstrong-Siddeley Siskin II (he meant Siskin III) from June 1924. The Siskin III continued until late 1926 when it was replaced by the Siskin IIIA.

It's hard to assess this information, because there are no photographs of Treble-One's Grebes and no recorded serials. Thompson and Sturtivant's detailed and comprehensive record of Royal Air Force serials from

J1 to J9999, which covers every Grebe that was built, lists but a single Grebe which served with the squadron, but it's a two-seater Grebe IIIDC and it didn't arrive until January 1928, long after the squadron re-equipped with the Siskin IIIA. If anyone can provide documentary evidence of 111 Squadron's Grebes the author would be pleased to hear from them.

Grebe II J7413 of 56 Squadron, where it served from December 1924 to October 1926 apart from a few days at Farnborough in June 1926. It was later converted to dual control and was with 25 Squadron from July 1928 for a year, except for a brief spell at Martlesham. (Via Jack Meaden)

56 Squadron

The first squadron fully equipped with the Grebe was 56 Squadron, based at Biggin Hill, which received its aircraft in September 1924 as replacements for the Snipe. It operated its Grebes until September 1927, when they were succeeded by the Siskin IIIA. When colourful squadron markings were introduced 56 Squadron adopted red and white checks.

Engine run-up in an unidentified Grebe of 56 Squadron in 1927. (Via JD Oughton)

The squadron had three Commanding Officers during the time it was equipped with Grebes. Squadron Leader Sir Quintin (or Christopher, as he was known at the time) Brand KBE DSO MC DFC was CO when 56 Squadron received its new Grebes. He had been in the news in early 1920 as co-pilot of the first flight from Britain to South Africa. He and his colleague set off in a Vickers Vimy named the Silver Queen. It crashed in Egypt but Brand and his colleague pressed on in another Vimy and, when that crashed at Bulawayo, in a DH9. In May 1925 Squadron Leader FJ Vincent DFC took over command of the squadron and from September 1926 the CO was Squadron Leader CH Elliott AFC.

Grebe II J7583 served with no less than four different fighter squadrons. It was first with 19 Squadron, went to 29 Squadron in August 1925, to 56 Squadron the following October and ended up with 25 Squadron, where it was recorded in December 1927. (Via JD Oughton)

25 Squadron

25 Squadron at Hawkinge followed a month later and was soon recognised as the finest of the Grebe squadrons, nicknamed The Cuckoos. It was equipped with Grebes from October 1924 to July 1929, longer than any other unit. They replaced the Snipe and were succeeded by the Siskin IIIA. Some sources refer to 25 Squadron as the first Grebe squadron, but this appears to be incorrect.

The squadron had no less than four commanding officers during this time: Squadron Leader AH Peck DSO MC until September 1926, Squadron Leader ED Atkinson DFC AFC until April 1927, Squadron Leader WH Park MC DFC until September 1928 and thereafter Squadron Leader LGS Payne MC AFC. At the 1926 RAF Display at Hendon, held on 3 July, Peck led a display of Grebes which manoeuvred to his instructions transmitted by radio-telephone. He would later become an Air Vice-Marshal. The Squadron markings were two parallel black bars.

GLOSTER GREBE
ONE ARMSTRONG SIDDELEY JAGUAR ENGINE

FLIGHT
International Photograph

One of the best known images of the Grebe, this Flight photograph shows two aircraft of 25 Squadron. Both pilots are flying with goggles but without helmets. (Flight photo, from author's collection)

Squadron visit: eight Grebe IIs of 25 Squadron lined up on Brockworth airfield. Serials include (from nearest) J7363, J7402, J7290, J729x and J7368. J7363 wears ID bands on the rear fuselage and the lower starboard wing as well as an X on the starboard cockpit coaming. (Author's collection)

An unidentified 25 Squadron Grebe II with the early, narrow-stripe squadron markings, mating with a Hucks starter. (Via Jack Meaden)

32 Squadron

32 Squadron at Kenley operated Grebes from November 1924 to January 1927. They replaced the Snipe and were succeeded by the Gloster Gamecock I. The first Gamecocks arrived in September 1926, well before the squadron relinquished its Grebes. Squadron Leader HP Lale DSO MC was CO until August 1926 when Squadron Leader (later Air Commodore) Reginald Baynes Mansell took over. Squadron colours were a broad blue bar with three diagonal breaks.

Grebe II J7571 in 32 Squadron markings at Kenley in 1927. After a brief spell with 29 Squadron that summer it was shipped to Hinaidi in Iraq for tropical trials, rebuilt as JR7571 and attached to 14 Squadron (then operating with DH9As) between May and October 1929. It stayed in the Middle East, was with No. 4 Flying Training School in 1930 and - as one of the last serving RAF Grebes - appeared in the Heliopolis Air Pageant in February 1931. (Via JD Oughton)

An unidentified 32 Squadron Grebe at RAF Cranwell. (Via JD Oughton)

J7361 in 32 Squadron's blue markings between 1925 and 1927. The fin also appears to be painted blue. It collided with a Bristol Fighter in June 1926, returning to the squadron after repairs at the Home Aircraft Depot. This aircraft later served with 25 Squadron, from June 1927 until February 1928. (Via Phil Butler)

Before adopting its better-known blue and white chequers 19 Squadron used this unusual design in blue. The aircraft is Grebe II J7390. It was with 19 Squadron between December 1925 and July 1926 (and recorded at the Armament & Gunnery School in April 1926) before being transferred to 29 Squadron. This aircraft later served with 25 Squadron, from June 1927 until February 1928. (Via Phil Butler)

19 Squadron

19 Squadron at Duxford was equipped with Grebes from December 1924 until April 1928. Yet again they replaced the Snipe and were followed by the Siskin IIIA. Squadron Leader P Babington MC AFC was CO until July 1925 and was followed by Squadron Leader HWG Jones MC. Early squadron colours consisted of two thin diagonal lines in opposite directions between two thin horizontal lines, all in blue, but the squadron soon adopted its better-known markings of large blue and white checks. There is a photo of the CO's aircraft, J7585, with check pennants attached to the rear interplane struts and to the rudder. Since this Grebe didn't join the squadron until 1927 it must be Squadron Leader Jones's aircraft.

22 Squadron

Aircraft at Martlesham were officially part of 22 Squadron but this was not a service squadron.

Two Grebes wearing the blue and white chequers of 19 Squadron, probably belonging to A Flight. Photographed at Duxford in 1927, they include J7368 (left). (Author's collection)

A Grebe of 19 Squadron, with two Bristol Fighters in the background. (via Phil Butler)

29 Squadron

The last squadron to equip with Grebes was 29 Squadron at Duxford, which received its aircraft in January 1925, again replacing the Snipe. In March 1928 they were succeeded by the Siskin IIIA. Commanding Officers at the time were Squadron Leader RHG Neville MC until August 1927, followed by Squadron Leader ML Taylor AFC. Squadron colours were four red Xs with narrow red bars above and below (the squadron later changed its markings to three red Xs on its Siskins and two on its Bulldogs).

An unidentified Grebe of 29 Squadron with underwing bomb racks fitted. The tail of Siskin III J7149 can be seen on the left. (Via Phil Butler)

Grebe II J7381 of 29 Squadron photographed at Duxford in 1926. It left the squadron in August that year and was later sold to New Zealand as NZ501. (Via JD Oughton)

Grebe II J7571 during its short time with 29 Squadron in 1927, with XXX squadron markings rather than the usual four. It is followed by a Grebe of 25 Squadron, probably at Hendon. (Photo by RW Walker, via Jet Age Museum)

Grebe II J7380 of 29 Squadron overturned on landing at Cranwell in July 1925. It had been with the squadron since January that year. The photo gives a good view of the bomb carriers. (Via JD Oughton)

Grebe II J7393 joined 29 Squadron in September 1925 but came to grief when landing at Duxford the following year. It's hard to believe that it was rebuilt, but it was briefly with 56 Squadron in December 1927-January 1928. (Via JD Oughton).

"Hallo mosquitoes"

The annual RAF display at Hendon attracted large crowds of spectators and was the perfect showcase for the Grebe. Formation aerobatics were already a popular spectacle but the 1925 display introduced something new: HM King George V giving order by wireless to 25 Squadron's Grebes.

Nine Grebes carried out a variety of complex manoeuvres, then their leader, Squadron Leader AH Peck, signalled "*awaiting His Majesty's order*".

"*Hallo mosquitoes!*" the King replied. "*Alter course 16 points outwards!*" ("*mosquitoes*" was the call sign of the day for aircraft in the air). Flight magazine reported: "*Immediately the leader executed a loop and half roll from the top, while the others turned sharply in the reverse direction, and there was the formation once again in double line ahead, but flying in the opposite direction*". The occasion was broadcast across the nation by the British Broadcasting Company.

HM King George V directs Grebe manoeuvres by wireless. (From the 1927 Wonder Book of Aircraft, author's collection)

Grebes "in action"

The nearest the Grebe ever came to seeing action was in the three-day Army Manoeuvres of September 1925. No air-to-air combat was involved, but the Grebes of 25 and 56 Squadrons were used to some effect on troops and armour.

"The Cuckoos" (25 Squadron) were led by Squadron Leader AH Peck DSO MC. Major Robertson of Flight reported that at one stage "*there were nine Grebes of No 25 tearing up in squadron mass. The hedges of the road were low and afforded no cover. The squadron changed into circular formation over the heads of the devoted infantry, and fell upon their prey in scientific fashion. Now from one direction and now from another in rapid succession, Grebe after Grebe dived on the Berkshires, shooting and bombing, and then zoomed up to its place in the wheeling circle*". Later that day they found Earl Haig and a group of foreign attachés "*and performed the same manoeuvre over them, just to show how British aircraft do it*". At another stage in the manoeuvres two flights from the squadron set upon the 7th Hussars.

Squadron Leader FJ Vincent DFC led 56 Squadron. He had just taken over as CO from his distinguished predecessor Squadron Leader Sir Christopher Brand KBE DSO MC DFC, who had been posted to the Air Ministry Supply and Research Department on the eve of the exercises. One flight of 56 Squadron "*caught the 4th Guards Brigade on the march and delivered a rapid attack*".

A Grebe of 25 Squadron with engine failure had to land on very rough ground and was badly damaged, the pilot escaping with minor injuries. Two Grebes from 56 Squadron made forced landings behind the "enemy" lines, one of them crashing, and both pilots were taken prisoner.

All in all, though, the two fighter squadrons proved to be extremely effective and the smartness of 25 Squadron in particular was remarked on: "*... my colleague saw No. 25 Squadron waiting for orders on its aerodrome one morning, the machines out ready and the pilots in their flying clothes even to their gloves. The orders came, and in exactly eight minutes the three flights were in the air. Smart work that!*"

An intriguing postscript appeared in Flight more than 20 years later. Capt RT Shepherd, chief test pilot of Rolls-Royce, recalled flying into the ground when he was "outside man" in a flight of five Grebes in the Air Exercises of 1925 - this seems to be a reference to the Army Manoeuvres. He said that he "*turned over endways three times - and then stepped out*".

In 1962 the great Flight photographer John Yoxall, who was there to photograph the manoeuvres, remarked: "*The incredible thing that struck one was that the Army, after experiencing five years of mechanised slaughter, was still adhering firmly to the employment of cavalry*".

Other Grebes in RAF service

After the Gamecock replaced the Grebe in squadron service, formation aerobatics by Grebes of 22 Squadron from Martlesham featured in the annual RAF Display from 1929 to 1931, giving way to Bulldogs the following year. The three Grebes in the 1931 display were flown by Flight Lieutenants DM Fleming, CB Wincott and JR Adams. They made spectacular loops, criss-crosses and spirals and formed "Prince of Wales' feathers" in white and orange smoke using apparatus supplied by Major Jack Savage. Upper wing and tailplane surfaces, the fin and the top of the fuselage were painted scarlet.

J7587, already languishing in Martlesham's dump, ended its days in 1931 when the Establishment used it to test an Essex model fire extinguisher.

Grebe two-seaters

Although the RAF did not order the Grouse as a trainer, as Gloster had hoped, it did order a two-seat trainer version of the Grebe itself, known as the Grebe IIIDC. John WR Taylor described the Grebe trainer with its 150 mph top speed as 20 mph faster than many RAF fighters.

When the first two-seater Grebe was tested at Martlesham, the pilot, Flt Lt HV Rowley, nearly came to grief. He initiated a spin at 15,000 feet but when he tried to recover above 10,000 feet the aircraft did not respond.

J7519 was the first production two-seater Grebe IIIDC. Seen here at Brockworth, it first flew on 6 July 1924, going to Martlesham later the same month. It came back to Gloster to be fitted with anti-flutter struts, returned to Martlesham for performance trials between May 1925 and February 1927 and competed in the 1929 King's Cup Air Race. It was then transferred to 23 Squadron and was written off on 17 March 1930 when it bounced and overturned on landing at Farnborough. (Via JD Oughton)

He only managed to regain control at 4,000 feet after resorting to the drastic use of full throttle and with the control column fully forward. The pilot in the rear seat was a tall man and his height was evidently enough to blank the Grebe's rudder.

Twenty aircraft were built as Grebe trainers, but a handful of others were converted from single-seaters: known examples are J7400 (for New Zealand), J7413 and J7585.

King's Cup winner

An unidentified Grebe IIIDC with extra vee interplane struts. (Author's collection)

Grebe two-seaters were entered in the 1928 and 1929 King's Cup air race. Gloster achieved welcome publicity in July 1929 when J7520 won the race. The company splashed out on a full centre spread in Flight magazine. Flight Lieutenant RL Atcherley flew the Grebe to victory in the two-day race, with Flight Lieutenant GH Stainforth as his navigator. The aircraft was entered in the race by Sir Walter Preston, Member of Parliament for Cheltenham, with the pilot listed under the pseudonym R Llewellyn, presumably to confound the bookies. The advertisement quoted the Daily Telegraph: "*The winner's average speed over the whole course of 1,176 miles (1893 km) was 150.3 miles per hour (241.9 km/h). This is a record for the King's Cup. ... The incredible had happened, and the Grebe, which had been 42 minutes behind the leader at Leeds, and 27 minutes behind him at Birmingham, had overtaken him and four others in the last short lap*".

It was indeed a remarkable win. Some time after seeing all the competing aircraft off on the last leg of the Friday's race, from Bristol to Blackpool, works manager Frank McKenna received a telegram from Atcherley:

Grebe IIIDC J7520 with racing number 23, seconded from Central Flying School for the 1929 King's Cup Air Race, which it won. It had previously served with 25 and 29 Squadrons. (Author's collection)

Dick Atcherley and George Stainforth in J7520 taxi in immediately after winning the 1929 King's Cup Air Race. (Author's collection)

"*Damaged rudder, fin and tailskid landing at Blackpool. Any hope of repairs?*" It was 7.00 pm and McKenna was 200 miles away. He telephoned ahead to Brockworth to ask them to prepare the tail unit of Gloster's civil demonstrator Grebe G-EBHA and got back there as soon as he could. With two helpers, he then set off at 11 pm "*armed with the spares, plus tool kits, nuts and bolts, screws, glue, fabric and dope ... in the firm's Austin 12, fortified with bread and cheese and bottles of beer.*" They drove through a thunderstorm at Whitchurch, got lost in Warrington and eventually arrived at Squire's Gate at 4.30 am. Luckily "*practically every bolt hole picked up and the new rudder, fin and tailskid were duly fitted to the aircraft by 8.30 am, Atcherley being due to take off at 9.55*". They worked until daylight using lamps borrowed from the Salvation Army and their "workshop" was "*a fence on which the tail end of the fuselage rested.*" Unsurprisingly, this was the month when the six year-old G-EBHA was withdrawn from use.

A second Grebe entered in the race was piloted by EH "Mouse" Fielden (later to be Captain of the King's Flight) with the elderly Hon Freddie Guest as passenger. Their aircraft suffered a broken flying wire and had to land for repairs, but still managed to come in seventh.

Atcherley (left) and Stainforth face the crowds after their surprise win. (Via Jet Age Museum)

The last Grebes left squadron service in the same month, prompting CG Grey, the caustic editor of The Aeroplane, to write of the 1929 King's Cup race: "*To see people entering ancient things like Grebes and SE5As would be funny if it were not so tragic.*"

George Stainforth piloted the Gloster VI seaplane to a new but short-lived world speed record of 336 mph later the same year and Atcherley and Stainforth both became world speed record holders in Supermarine seaplanes. Stainforth lost his life some years later in an air accident in the Middle East, while Air Marshal Sir Richard Atcherley (1904-1970) retired from the RAF in 1959 and was sales director of Folland Aircraft until 1965.

Navy Grebes

Three Grebe IIIDCs and later three Grebe IIs were loaned by the RAF for use at naval shore establishments. The two-seaters J7521, 7525 and 7529 served at the RAF Training Base at Leuchars at various dates between October 1925 and March 1928. Single-seat Mk IIs J7396 and 7595 were also at Leuchars between late 1928 and early 1929, while J7585 was at RAF Base Gosport in late 1928.

Experimental Grebes

Experimental work carried out with Grebes bore a marked influence on later designs. Some of the experiments in which they were involved were as follows:

Terminal velocity

The company's in-house magazine "The Gloster" reported in its issue of January-February 1926: "*Two Grebes survive a drastic test - An experiment, which revealed equally the courage of British pilots and the excellence of*

Civil-registered Grebe G-EBHA was retained by the company as a demonstrator and used later for experimental work. Here it is seen at Brockworth with Jupiter engine, oleo undercarriage and Gamecock-type fin and rudder. (Author's collection)

Another shot of Grebe G-EBHA (Author's collection)

British aircraft design, was carried out recently at Martlesham aerodrome. Two pilots, equipped with the latest type of parachute, set out in Gloster 'Grebes' with the deliberate intention of breaking the machines in mid-air. Climbing to a height of about three miles they dived nearly vertically with engines full on. When the speed had reached about 240 miles per hour the pilots pulled hard on their respective control levers and flattened out. This operation brings such huge strains on the structure that the pilots each expected their wings to break and were prepared to make a hurried exit, relying on their parachutes for safety. Much to their astonishment nothing broke and they were able to make a perfectly normal landing. Careful examination of the machines revealed that the only adjustment necessary was the slight operation of tightening up some of the bracing wires which had stretched under the terrific loads imposed upon them. Viva la Grebe!"

One of the pilots was Flight Lieutenant D D'Arcy Greig DFC AFC and the Grebes were fitted with experimental aileron modifications and extra outer wing struts. The terminal velocity test was the first of its kind and could only be considered because the first Irvin parachutes were now available. On 22 April 1927, flying from Kenley, D'Arcy Greig escaped from an uncontrollable spin in another Grebe and became the fourth member of the RAF's Caterpillar Club.

VP airscrew

Gloster's own Grebe, the civil-registered G-EBHA, was used as a company demonstrator in 1923 and was displayed, alongside its Grouse predecessor, at the Gothenburg International Aeronautical Exhibition in Sweden, flying there a few days after its first flight. No Swedish order for the Grebe was forthcoming, but the Swedish Army did buy the single example of the Grouse for use as a trainer. G-EBHA was later fitted with the Mk II's oleo undercarriage and in 1926 with a 425 hp (317 kW) Bristol Jupiter IV radial engine with open exhausts and the Gamecock's taller, counterbalanced rudder. In this form it was used to test the Hele Shaw-Beacham variable-pitch propeller developed by an in-house team of the Gloster company led by "Pop" Milner. The Gamecock was also used to test variable-pitch propellers.

G-EBHA, now with three-part windscreen, went on to be used for the first flight tests of the Gloster-built Hele-Shaw Beacham VP propeller. The pilot is Howard Saint. Believed to be Flight photographs. (Author's collection, above and via JD Oughton, below))

The airship experiments

A notable experiment took place on 21 October 1926 when two Grebes were carried aloft by the airship R33 from Pulham airship station in Norfolk. They were both air-launched successfully from about 2,000 ft, one over Pulham, the other over the airship station at Cardington in Bedfordshire.

"*HM Air Aircraft Carrier R33*", as she was described in Flight, was used to demonstrate the practicability of aircraft "*to be transported speedily to distant parts and successfully launched*". The effect of suddenly releasing a sizeable load was also investigated: a pair of Grebes weighed in at 2.5 tons and between them they needed the lift of 80,000 cu ft of hydrogen out of the airship's total capacity of 2,000,000 cu ft.

R33 was the sister ship of the famous R34, which made the first two-way crossing of the Atlantic in 1919. It first flew that same year and was a copy of the downed Zeppelin L33. It had already been used to release a pilotless Camel over the North Yorkshire Moors in 1920 and in 1925 it was used to drop a DH53 Hummingbird, which managed to re-connect on the third attempt. It had a maximum speed of 62 mph and with a length of 643 ft it was almost 32 times longer than a Grebe.

Commanded by Maj GH Scott, R33 carried 35 people for the first Grebe trial, including the Director of Airship Development. The two Grebes, J7385 and J7400, were piloted by Flying Officers Robert Linton Ragg and C Mackenzie-Richards, both of the Royal Aircraft Establishment. Each Grebe hung from a central quick-release attachment with additional stabilising struts to the wings and rear fuselage. Flexible piping connected a Bristol gas starter inside the airship to each Grebe's Jaguar engine.

The pilots had to enter their cockpits via rope ladders from openings in the airship's keel. Equipped with parachutes, they did this during the flight, some 90 minutes after the airship was launched. Both had trouble starting their engines. Mackenzie-Richards got away first, Ragg not until almost an hour and a half later, with R33 travelling at about 30 mph. Both landed successfully. R33 landed at Cardington and in due course the Grebes were re-attached "*in readiness for a visit of the Dominions Premiers*".

Grebes J7400, seen here, and J7385 were used for the first air-launch trial with the airship R33 in 1926. The pilots had to climb down rope ladders in flight to enter the Grebes' cockpits. (Author's collection)

A second test took place on 23 November with two more Grebes, J7408 and J7587. Squadron Leader BE Baker piloted a Grebe released over Cardington and an unnamed pilot landed the second Grebe at Pulham.

Flying Officer Mackenzie-Richards was killed parachuting from an aircraft in November 1927, while Air Vice-Marshal Ragg CB CBE AFC became AOC No 18 Group, Coastal Command, retiring as Air Marshal in 1955. Air Vice-Marshal Sir Brian Baker KBE CB DSO MC AFC retired in 1950 as AOC-in-C RAF Transport Command. J7400 was later converted to dual control and sold to New Zealand (see below).

Other Grebe experiments

A number of other Grebe experiments were tried, according to Gloster company files.

In 1925 one was modified to take a single Vickers 0.50 in gun and another was fitted with a Colt machine gun, also of 0.50 calibre. In 1927-28 the so-called "Clear View Grebe" was an attempt to improve the pilot's view. Three versions were built: one with a thinned-down centre section, one with the upper wing roots curved downward to fair into the fuselage and one with the centre section "cut entirely away" leaving a two-foot gap. Tests were completed in July 1928. The third version gave *"the best speeds and climbs"* but the first gave the best all-round view and was incorporated in the three Grebes which were rebuilt for New Zealand. The author would be pleased to hear if photographs of any of these versions survive.

Gloster inspector Basil Fielding recalled: *"The Clear View Grebe Biplane - This aircraft as far as I can remember was a standard Grebe but fitted with a special centre section designed to give the pilot a better view forward. It tapered down in the centre to approximately 2" thickness. The aircraft was flown but never went into production and I believe only one was produced"*. We know from a letter written on 7 October 1927 by George Dowty, then a Gloster employee, that the Clear View Grebe was one of many jobs *"going through"* the drawing office on that date.

A Grebe with a supercharged Jaguar IV attained a top speed of 165 mph at 10,000 ft. It proved capable of climbing to 20,000 ft in 16 minutes and reached an absolute ceiling of 27,000 ft. The Grebe was also proposed as a test bed for the Rolls-Royce Condor V-12 in-line engine but company files state that this *"did not get beyond the drawing board"*.

This needs some amplification, though. An in-line engined version of the Grebe was in fact developed, using the Napier Lion, and was known as the Gloster Gorcock. It is usually regarded as a Gamecock variant, since the Gamecock prototype flew earlier than the first Gorcock, but the Gamecock and Gorcock were developed in parallel, at least initially. Photographs of Gorcock J7501 at Brockworth in 1925 show not only a Grebe-style fin and rudder but also what are clearly Grebe rather than Gamecock upper wings with tapering ailerons and Grebe-pattern fuel tanks. Indeed, Harald Penrose described the Gorcock as *"an experimental all-metal version of the Grebe"*. The Gorcock is described in more detail in its own section.

New Zealand Grebes

Three ex-RAF Grebes became in 1928 the first fighters of the five-year-old New Zealand Permanent Air Force - even though none of them were ever fitted with machine guns. The first was paid for by the gift of £2,500 by Sir Henry Wigram, who had urged the original formation of the NZPAF.

All three were ex-RAF machines, refurbished by the Gloster Aircraft Company and with parallel-chord ailerons and rounded wing tips. They also lacked the collector ring and extended exhausts of later RAF Grebes. NZ501 (ex-J7381) had served with 29 Squadron RAF from September 1925 to August 1926. It arrived in New Zealand in February 1928 and first flew on 2 March 1928, piloted by Wigram Base CO Capt JL Findlay. A series of test flights were then undertaken by Capt LM Isitt. Fitting a spinner increased its top speed by 5 mph.

New Zealand Grebe NZ501, formerly J7381, served with 29 Squadron RAF from September 1925 to August 1926. It arrived in New Zealand in February 1928. (Via Jet Age Museum)

NZ502 , which as J7394 served with 29 Squadron RAF from March 1925 until July 1926, was delivered on 23 September 1928. Grebe two-seater NZ503 was the former single-seater J7400 which had taken part in the first R33 airship trials in October 1926 as well as serving with 25 Squadron RAF. It was photographed at Gloster's Brockworth airfield in August 1928 being demonstrated in its New Zealand markings by chief test pilot Howard Saint and was delivered the following December.

NZ502 was damaged in November 1929, wrecking the starboard lower wing, and was later rebuilt, NZ503 was written off on 8 August 1932, diving into the ground from 1,000 ft after an elevator control rod broke. Pilot JL Findlay, now a squadron leader, and aircraftman J Simpson were severely injured.

J7400 turns up again, now rebuilt for New Zealand as two-seater NZ503. It was delivered in 1928. (Flight photo, Jet Age Museum)

Grebe NZ501 leads Bristol Fighters of the New Zealand Permanent Air Force. (Public domain, via Wikipedia)

New Zealand Grebe NZ501 was later re-numbered A-5 and was in service until 1938, when it became an instructional airframe. (Jet Age Museum/Russell Adams Collection)

NZ501 and NZ502, now re-numbered A-5 and A-6 respectively, last appeared in June 1938 at the now-Royal New Zealand Air Force's Rongotai pageant. They were withdrawn from use the following November and became Instructional Airframes No 2 and 3 at Hobsonville.

Flying the Grebe

The Grebe made an impression on RAF squadron pilots who flew it and it was a popular aerobatic mount with good performance for its day. Although very manoeuvrable, it was not tiring to fly as a lever in the cockpit controlling the adjustable tailplane allowed it to be trimmed to fly hands-off. It was difficult to handle near its stress limits, however, when it suffered from wing flutter.

Air Commodore Allen Wheeler wrote in Flight's Gloster 40th anniversary issue of 1965: "*In the Gloster range one had to go back as far as the Grebe to find that sense of being part of the aeroplane - the feeling that one could lean to one side and tilt it like a bicycle. But, if my memory is correct, the Grebe had only 365 hp. Though I had had only one flight in one - a met. climb to 20,000 ft - I well recall that lack of reserve of power as we approached the top of the climb, and more particularly because it was beginning to get dark on earth below. At that time the pilot certainly felt very much one with the aeroplane - and very much alone. But the Grebe was a delightful little aircraft to handle and even in the growing dusk on a first flight it gave one a sense of confidence.*"

Summary of Grebe mods

Retrospectively designated Grebe I, prototype Grebes had traditional V-strut undercarriages and were unarmed. The prominent fuel tanks under the upper wing were full chord, rounded at the front and tapering to the rear in plan view. The Jaguar engine was a Mark III of 350 hp (261 kW) with stub exhausts. The upper wing ailerons were tapered, with the hinge line raked forward towards the tip in plan view while the chord remained constant.

Production Grebes were designated Grebe II and were armed with twin Vickers 0.303 in (7.7 mm) machine guns on the forward fuselage top decking. Gloster's new oleo undercarriage was standard and a steerable tail skid was fitted. The upper wing fuel tanks were revised and simplified, now rectangular in plan and gently convex when viewed from the side. From February 1925 the ailerons were still raked forward but no longer tapered, resulting in a distinctive kink where the trailing edge of the aileron protruded beyond the trailing edge of the wing itself. The more powerful Jaguar IV of 400 hp (298 kW) was fitted. Other service equipment included wireless, navigation lights, Holt flare brackets and racks for four 25 lb (11.34 kg) Cooper bombs.

Modifications to RAF Grebes while in service included fitting the engine with a collector ring and a pair of long exhausts in 1926, the addition of outer interplane V-struts to deal with the problem of wing flutter and fitting low-pressure tyres. A non-standard mod adopted by 29 Squadron at Duxford in 1924 consisted of sawing six inches off the air intake pipes on each side of the fuselage to prevent carburettor icing. This was devised by FR Wynne, who as a retired group captain recalled his brainwave in a letter to Flight in 1971.

Apart from the extra cockpit, the two-seater, designated Grebe IIIDC, had un-raked parallel-chord ailerons on upper as well as lower wings.

All three New Zealand Grebes had un-raked parallel-chord ailerons and were not fitted with interplane V-struts. They had a thinner upper wing centre section than the Grebe II, apparently adopted after the Clear View Grebe experiments.

Grebe units

19 Squadron
J7284, J7294, J7357, J7358, J7368, J7372, J7373, J7374, J7375, J7376, J7377, J7378, J7386, J7387, J7389, J7390, J7391, J7396, J7397, J7407, J7408, J7417, J7524 (DC), J7525 (DC), J7526 (DC), J7528 (DC), J7530 (DC), J7531 (DC), J7532 (DC), J7568, J7569, J7572, J7574, J7577, J7578, J7579, J7580, J7583, J7585 (converted to DC), J7587, J7591, J7592, J7594, J7600, J7601.

25 Squadron
J7283 (service trials), J7284, J7285, J7286, J7287, J7288, J7289, J7290, J7291, J7292, J7293, J7294, J7358, J7360, J7361, J7363, J7365, J7368, J7370, J7372, J7374, J7379, J7384, J7385, J7392, J7400, J7402, J7406, J7407, J7409, J7410, J7411, J7412, J7413 (after conversion to DC), J7417, J7520 (DC), J7530 (DC), J7532 (DC), J7534 (DC), J7536 (DC), J7538 (DC), J7569, J7572, J7576, J7578, J7579, J7580, J7581, J7583, J7586, J7587, J7588, J7589, J7591, J7602, J7603, J7786.

29 Squadron
J7292, J7293, J7362, J7369, J7380, J7381, J7382, J7385, J7386, J7387, J7390, J7391, J7393, J7394, J7395, J7396, J7397, J7520 (DC), J7521 (DC), J7527 (DC), J7528 (DC), J7532 (DC), J7533 (DC), J7538 (DC), J7570, J7571, J7576, J7583, J7585 (converted to DC), J7591, J7592, J7593, J7595, J7596, J7597, J7598, J7784, J7785, J7786.

32 Squadron
J7360, J7361, J7365, J7369, J7371, J7399, J7526 (DC), J7570, J7571, J7586, J7588, J7599, J7601.

56 Squadron
J7283 (service trials), J7289, J7290, J7357, J7358, J7359, J7385, J7393, J7397, J7401, J7406, J7407, J7408, J7409, J7410, J7411, J7412, J7413, J7414, J7415, J7416, J7417, J7522 (DC), J7535 (DC), J7573, J7582, J7583, J7584, J7585 (converted to DC), J7587.

Limited use by other squadrons: 3 Squadron: J7527 (DC). 23 Squadron: J7526 (DC), J7527 (DC). 43 Squadron: J7532 (DC). 111 Squadron: only recorded serial is J7524 (DC).

Flying Training Schools
2 FTS: J7382, J7417. 3 FTS: J7383. 4 FTS: see tropical trials below. 5 FTS: J7537 (DC).

Armament & Gunnery School
J7365, J7367, J7369, J7390, J7397, J7402, J7530 (DC), J7579, J7581, J7595, J7603, J7536 (DC).

Central Flying School: J7382, J7383, J7406, J7417, J7520 (DC), J7585 (converted to DC), J7599, J7600.

Met Flight, Duxford: J7371.

R33 airship trials: J7385, J7400, J7408, J7587.

RAF Cadet College: J7391.

Training Bases: Gosport: J7568, J7585. Leuchars: J7521 (DC), J7525 (DC), J7529 (DC), J7396, J7595.

Tropical trials: J7571 (RAF Hinaidi, attached 14 Squadron; 4 Flying Training School), J7593 (attached 4 Flying Training School, 14 Squadron, 216 Squadron).

1 School of Technical Training: J7415 (as instructional airframe).

Grebe contracts

Grebes first featured in the Gloucestershire Aircraft Company's accounts in their financial year 1923-24, which ended on 5 May. The company received £5000 for two experimental machines, presumably J6969 and J6970, and a further £199 for spares.

A grand total of 133 Grebes were built by the Gloucestershire/Gloster Aircraft Company, all in the three financial years 1923-26. Contracts for spares, reconditioning, modifications and experimental work meant that the company received a total of £585,029 for its Grebes and associated work over the seven-year period ending on 5 May 1930. The details are as follows:

Year ended:					
5 May 1924	2 machines	£5,000	Experimental	£2,500 each	
	Spares	£199	Spares		
5 May 1925	107 machines	£258,111	Production	£2,412 each	
	Spares	£35,994	Spares		
5 May 1926	24 machines	£55,050	Production	£2,294 each	
	15 machines	£19,760	Reconditioning	£1,317 each	
	Spares	£41,727	Spares		
5 May 1927	18 machines	£21,375	Reconditioning	£1,187 each	
	Spares	£56,527	Spares		
	Modifications	£3,318	Modifications		
5 May 1928	1 machine	£2,735	Experimental	£2,735	
	44 machines	£65,215	Reconditioning	£1,482 each	
	Spares	£9,089	Spares		
5 May 1929	2 machines	£5,675	Experimental	£2,837 each	
	Spares	£2,222	Spares		
	Modifications	£1,280	Modifications		
5 May 1930	Spares	£1,340	Spares		
	Modifications	£412	Modifications		
	Sub-totals	£13,410	Prototypes and experimental (5)		
		£313,161	Production (131)		
		£147,098	Spares		
		£106,350	Reconditioning (77)		
		£5,010	Modifications		
	TOTAL	£585,029			

Total Grebe production is recorded as 133, which tallies with the figures given above for the years ended May 1924, 1925 and 1926. The three additional experimental Grebes listed above as built in 1927-28 and 1928-29 are too late for any recorded RAF-serialled Grebe. They do fit in with deliveries of the three New Zealand Grebes, although they were not new machines but reconditioned RAF ones.

Grebe production summary

Total production 133

Grebe Mk I
Three prototype aircraft: J6969, J6970 and J6971
Ordered under Contract No 402023/23 dated 21 February 1923 as "Nighthawk with thick wing section".
To Specification 3/23. File No 406052/23.
Powered by 350 hp Armstrong Siddeley Jaguar III engine.
Built by Gloucestershire Aircraft Company during 1923. First flown May 1923.

J6969 First flown in May 1923 *"and taking part in the Hendon Air Pageant in June, it proved to be some 30 mph faster than contemporary types."* To AEE 22 June 1923. Hendon Display (number "14") on 30 June 1923. To RAE 24 July 1923. Instrument tests, later heated clothing. Back to GAC March 1924. To RAE again on 16 April 1924. General tests and high altitude tests. Last flown 24 August 1925.
J6970 To AEE from July 1923 to February 1924. Consumption tests, later comparison with Siskin for handling and manoeuvrability. Back to GAC March 1925. A&AEE (22 Squadron) 25 February 1926 to April 1927.
J6971 To A&AEE. Back to GAC August 1924.
One company demonstrator G-EBHA. First flew 6 July 1923 piloted by Larry Carter. C of A issued 11 July 1923.

Grebe Mk II
109 Grebe single-seat fighters powered by 400 hp Armstrong-Siddeley Jaguar IV with serials as follows:
J7283 - J7294 (12 aircraft). Contract number 468248/23 dated March 1924 .
J7357 - J7402 (46 aircraft). Contract number 511658/24 Part 1.
J7406 - J7417 (12 aircraft). Contract number 498862/24.
J7568 - J7603 (36 aircraft). Contract number 547417/24 Part 1.
J7784 - J7786 (3 aircraft). Contract number 547417/24 Part 2.

Grebe IIIDC
20 dual control Grebe trainers, serials J7519 - J7538
Ordered on Contract number 511658/24 Part 2, to be fitted with 400 hp Armstrong Siddeley Jaguar IV.
In addition, three single-seaters were converted to dual control: J7400 (for New Zealand), J7413 and J7585.

New Zealand Grebes

J7381 served with 29 Squadron RAF from September 1925 to August 1926. It was sold to New Zealand as NZ501 and first flew there on 2 March 1928. Later re-numbered A-5, it was withdrawn from use in November 1938 and became Instructional Airframe No 2.
J7394 served with 29 Squadron RAF from March 1925 until July 1926. It was sold to New Zealand as NZ502 and was delivered on 23 September 1928. Re-numbered A-6, it was withdrawn from use in November 1938 and became Instructional Airframe No 3.
J7400 went to Martlesham in February 1925 and to Farnborough on 14 September 1926. A week later it went to Pulham for trials with the airship R33. It entered service with 25 Squadron RAF on 25 January 1927 but in due course was converted into a dual control trainer and sold to New Zealand as NZ503, being delivered in December 1928. It crashed at Hornby on 8 August 1932 after an elevator control rod fractured.

Grebe details

Single seat fighter to Specification 3/23. Three Grebe I service prototypes, one civil demonstrator, 109 Grebe II, 20 Grebe IIIDC and three modified RAF Grebes for New Zealand.

Construction: wooden wings and fuselage, fabric covered.

Engine:
Grebe I: 350 hp (261 kW) Jaguar III
Grebe II, IIIDC and New Zealand Grebe: 400 hp (298 kW) Jaguar IV with 9 ft 6 in (2.9 m) dia. Watts propeller. G-EBHA later fitted with 455 hp (339 kW) Jupiter VI with 9 ft 10 in (3.0 m) dia. Gloster Hele-Shaw Beacham VP metal propeller.
One Grebe with 460 hp (343 kW) supercharged Jaguar IV with 9 ft 10 in (3.0 m) Watts propeller.

Armament: two .303 (7.7 mm) Vickers Mk I machine guns on top of the forward fuselage. Provision for four 20 lb (9 kg) Cooper bombs on two underwing racks or one rack under fuselage.

Dimensions: Span upper wing 29 ft 4 in (8.94 m), lower wing 25 ft (7.62 m). Length 20 ft 3 in (6.17 m). Height 9 ft 3 in (2.82 m). Wing area 254 sq ft (23.6 sq m).

Performance and weights:
Grebe I: top speed 151 mph (243 km/h) at 5,000 ft (1524 m). Climb to 5,000 ft (1524 m) 12.5 min. Service ceiling 23,000 ft (7010 m). Weight loaded 2622 lb (1189 kg), tare 1720 lb (780 kg).

Grebe II: top speed 162 mph (261 km/h) at sea level. Climb to 20,000 ft (6096 m) 24 min. Service ceiling 23,500 ft (7163 m). Weight loaded 2538 lb (1151 kg), tare 1695 lb (769 kg).
Grebe IIIDC: top speed 150 mph (241 km/h). Weight loaded 2576 lb (1168 kg).
Grebe G-EBHA (Jupiter): rate of climb improved by 200 ft/min (61 m/min).
New Zealand Grebe: top speed 162 mph (261 km/h). Climb to 15,000 ft (4572 m) 12 min. Service ceiling 23,000 ft (7010 m). Weight loaded 2538 lb (1151 kg).
Grebe (supercharged Jaguar): top speed 165 mph (266 km/h) at 10 000 ft (3048 m). Climb to 20,000 ft (6096 m) 16 min. Absolute ceiling 27,000 ft (8230 m).

Gloster's factory at Sunningend, Cheltenham, not far from the main railway station. In 1922 it had an extensive timber yard and a couple of ex-WW1 canvas Bessoneaux hangars. The large building in the centre housed the main production and assembly shops as well as the craft workshops of HH Martyn & Co. The design office was in the tall building front right. Many of the buildings still exist on what is now the Lansdown Industrial Estate. (Via Jet Age Museum)

Dope girls at work on Grebe wings at Sunningend. Health and safety measures in an atmosphere thick with organic solvents involved the girls drinking a pint of milk on each shift and having a fortnightly medical check. (Via Jet Age Museum)

Grebe wing assembly shop at Sunningend. (Via Jet Age Museum)

Grebe fuselage and wing assembly at Sunningend. The one visible serial, J7533, is for a two-seater Grebe IIIDC which served with 29 Squadron between May 1925 and January 1926. (Via Jet Age Museum)

Grebe undercarriages being made at Sunningend. (Via Jet Age Museum)

Grebe structure details

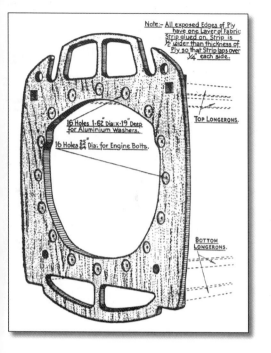

Note:- All exposed Edges of Ply have one Layer of Fabric Strip glued on. Strip is ½" wider than thickness of Ply so that Strip laps over ¼" each side.

16 Holes 1·62" Dia: x·19" Deep for Aluminium Washers.

16 Holes 29/64" Dia: for Engine Bolts.

TOP LONGERONS.

BOTTOM LONGERONS.

Engine bearer bulkhead.

22 G. Aluminium Plates

1/8" Asbestos.

Fireproof bulkhead.

Instrument board bulkhead.

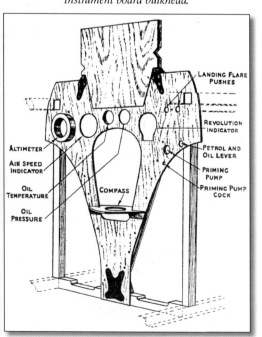

LANDING FLARE PUSHES

REVOLUTION INDICATOR

PETROL AND OIL LEVER

PRIMING PUMP

PRIMING PUMP COCK

ALTIMETER

AIR SPEED INDICATOR

OIL TEMPERATURE

OIL PRESSURE

COMPASS

Seat bearer bulkhead.

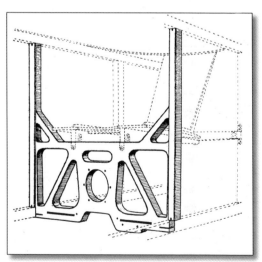

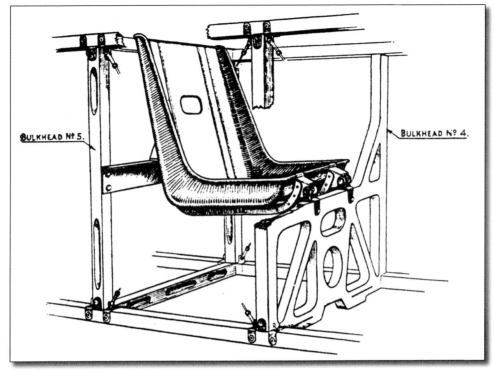

Seat.

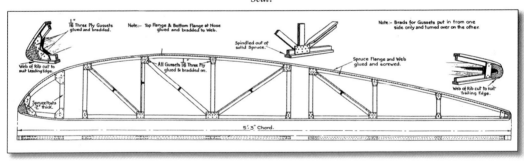

Standard rib for top main plane.

Standard rib for top bottom plane.

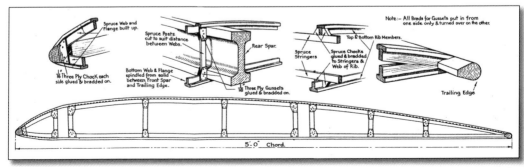

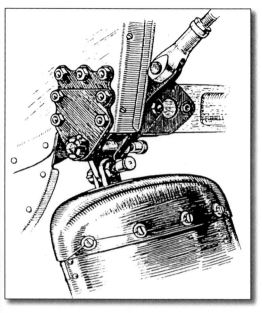

Attachment of oleo leg to fuselage.

Axle fitting.

Details of struts.

Tail skid.

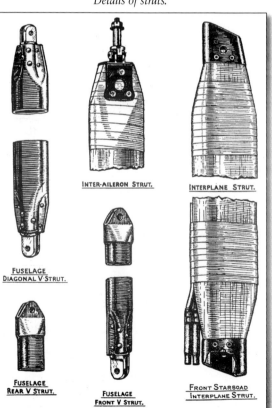

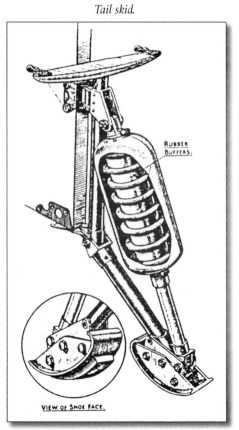

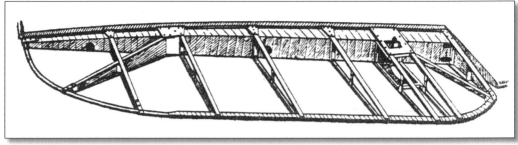

Top aileron.

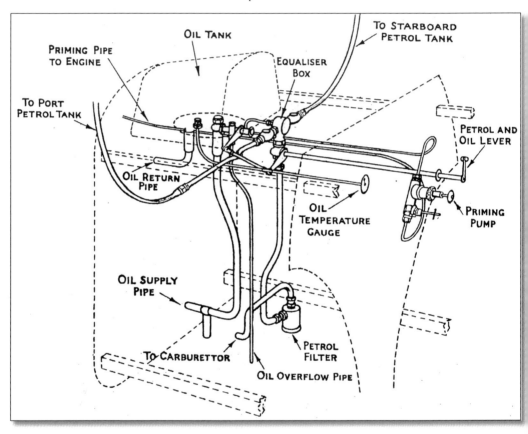

Petrol and oil systems.

Adjustment for rudder control.

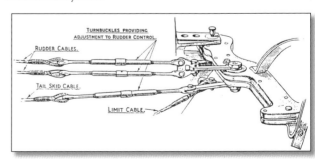

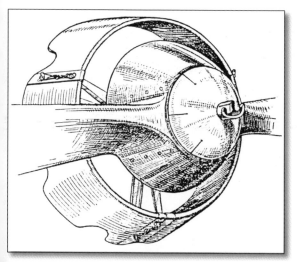

Engine cowling.

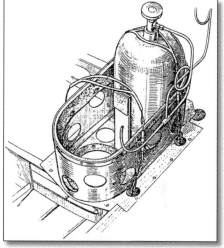

Oxygen cylinder container.

Windscreen.

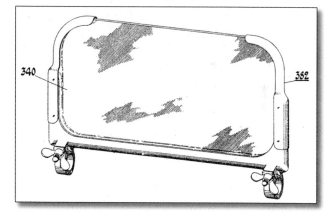

Control column.

Aldis sight brackets in position.

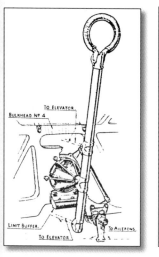

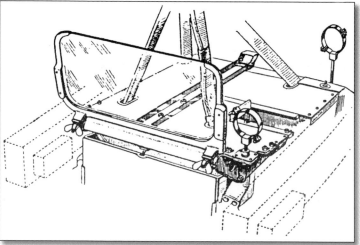

Instrument board.

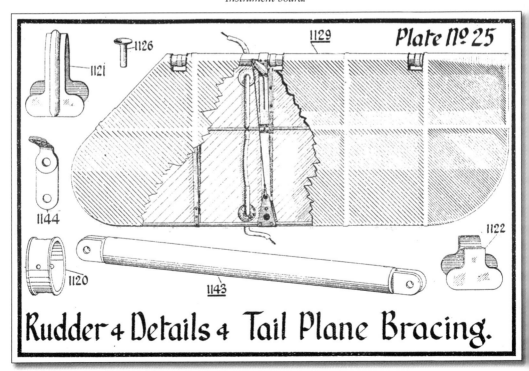

Plate № 25

Rudder ♦ Details ♦ Tail Plane Bracing.

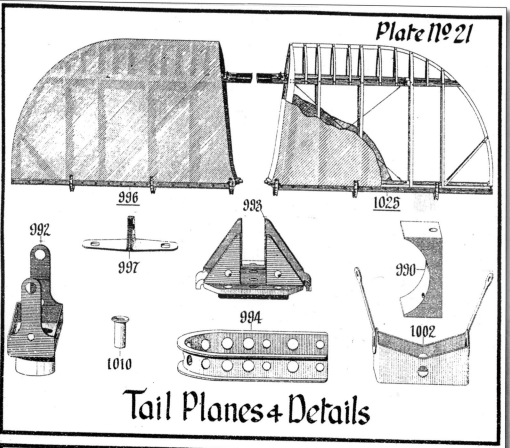

Plate № 21

996

1025

992

997

993

990

1010

994

1002

Tail Planes & Details

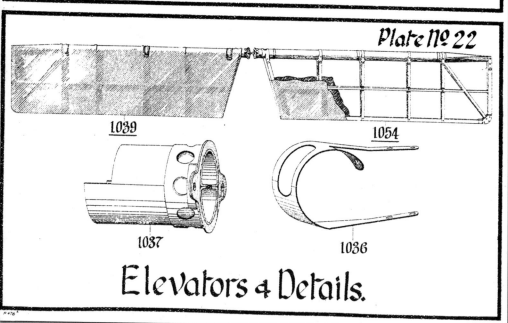

Plate № 22

1039

1054

1037

1036

Elevators & Details.

A rare photograph of the Grebe cockpit, with prominent gun breeches and central map case. (Via Jet Age Museum)

Grebe propeller boss. The stamped lettering reads "DRG No F3567/3 JAGUAR GREBE".

Grebe propeller boss from the rear, showing construction

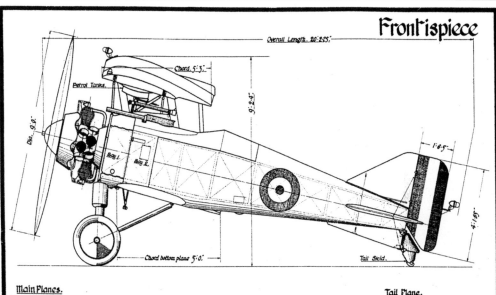

Frontispiece

Overall Length. 20.2.5.

Chord. 5.3.

Petrol Tanks.

9.2.4.5

Dia. 9.9.

Bay I. Bay II.

1.6.5.

4.1.0.5.

Chord bottom plane 5.0.

Tail Skid.

Main Planes.

Incidence, top plane	3°
Incidence, bottom plane	2°
Stagger	19.9.1"
Total area	254 sq ft.

Ailerons.

Span, top	5.10.5
Chord, top	15.5"
Area, top	9 sq ft.
Span, bottom	5.10.4"
Chord, bottom	15"
Area, bottom	7 sq ft.

Tail Plane.

Span	9'
Chord	2.5"
Total Area	18 sq ft
(less elevators)	
Range of incidence	-4° to 2°

Elevators.

Span	9'
Chord	1.5"
Total Area	10 sq ft

Oil . . . . 5½ galls.

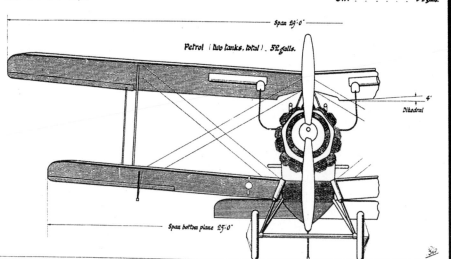

Span 29.0"

Petrol (two tanks, total) 52 galls.

4°
Dihedral

Span bottom plane 25.0"

Grebe Aeroplane.

Technical drawings

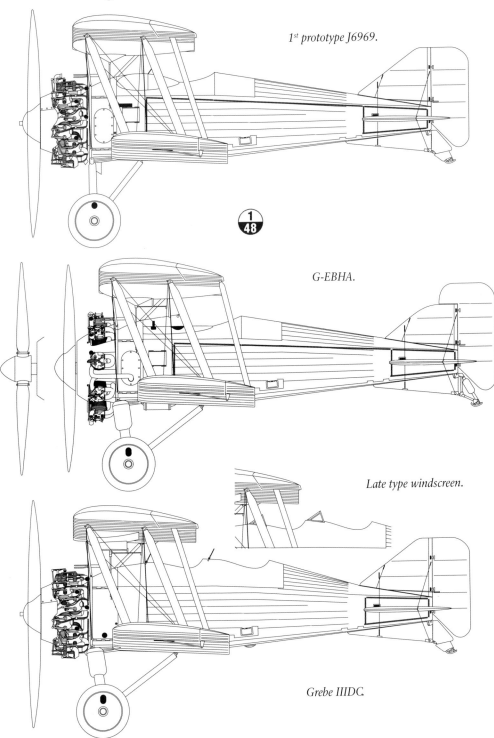

1ˢᵗ prototype J6969.

G-EBHA.

Late type windscreen.

Grebe IIIDC.

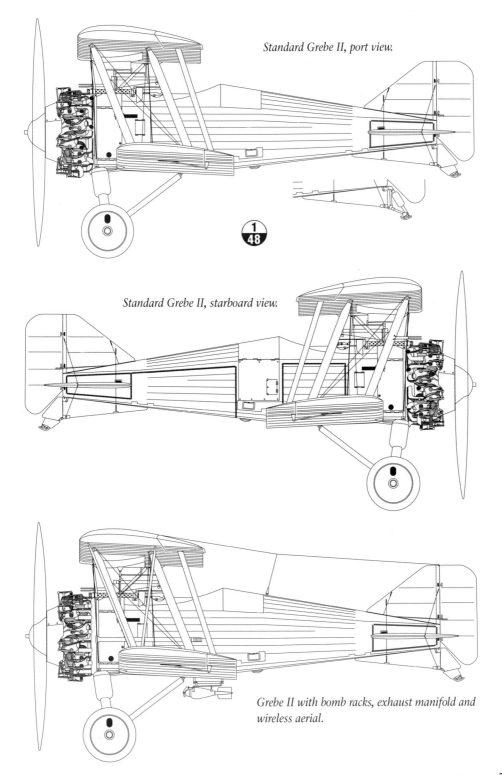

Standard Grebe II, port view.

Standard Grebe II, starboard view.

Grebe II with bomb racks, exhaust manifold and wireless aerial.

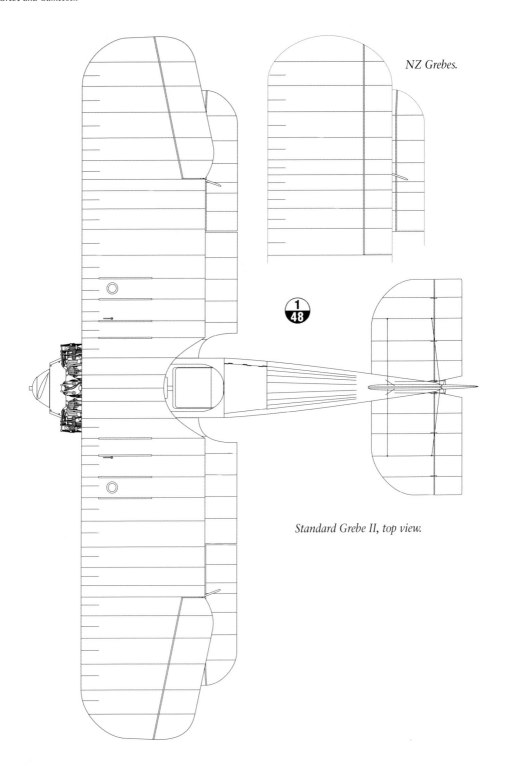

NZ Grebes.

Standard Grebe II, top view.

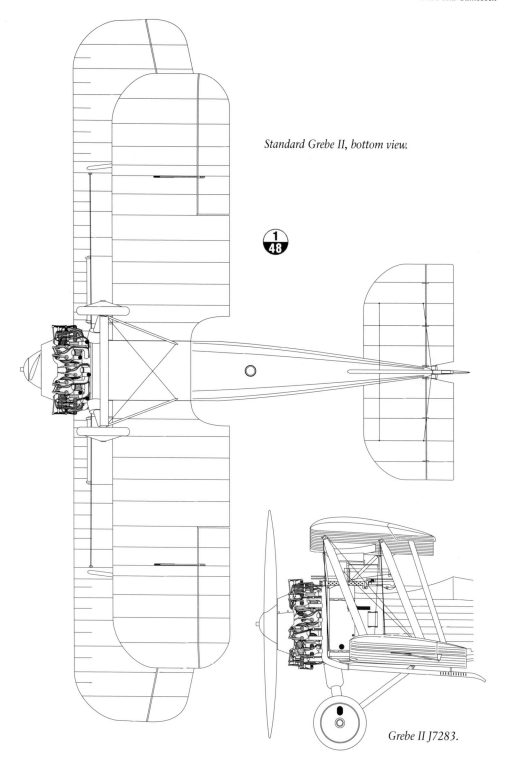

Standard Grebe II, bottom view.

Grebe II J7283.

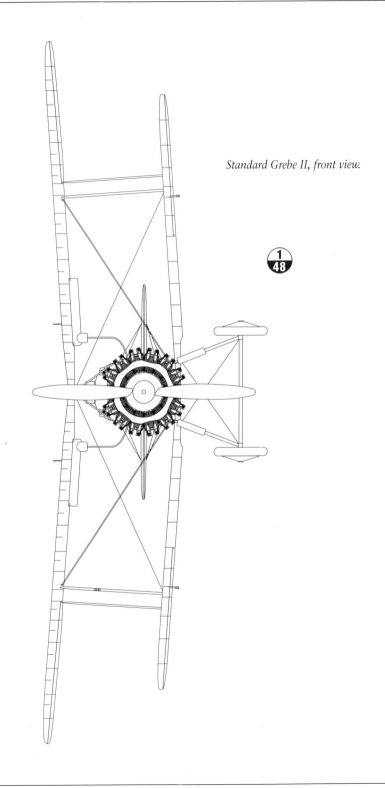

Standard Grebe II, front view.

Gamecock

Gamecock prototype

The Gamecock of 1925 was the natural successor to the Grebe once Roy Fedden's Bristol Jupiter radial had proved itself. The Jupiter gave more power than the Grebe's Jaguar for less weight, was simpler (with nine cylinders rather than fourteen), more reliable and easier to maintain. Moreover, Fedden was a vigorous promoter of his Jupiter design and was based at Filton, not that far from the Gloster works. Indeed, Fedden and Folland struck up a close and lasting working relationship and Fedden's Bristol radials would power many of Folland's future designs, including the RAF's Gauntlet and Gladiator.

Folland was also working on another Grebe development, powered by the Napier Lion in-line engine. This was to become the Gloster Gorcock, described in its own section.

An early version of the Jupiter had already been installed in the Nighthawk in 1922, first in J2405 at Farnborough in February/March and later in Mars VI Nighthawks J6926 and J6927 at Gloucestershire's Sunningend Works in November. The next step was to install a Jupiter in the company's Grebe civil demonstrator G-EBHA. This led to the Air Ministry ordering three prototype "Grebe II" aircraft to Specification 37/23: J7497, J7756 and J7757. The Grebe II designation, however, was then given to the Jaguar IV-powered Grebe, the RAF version,

Gamecock prototype J7497 photographed at Brockworth in its earliest configuration, still with Grebe-style fin and rudder. It first flew there in February 1925 before going to Martlesham. (Author's collection)

Another shot of the J7497 in its first configuration. (Via Jet Age Museum)

Back at Gloster around March 1925, Gamecock prototype J7497 was fitted with the new fin and rudder which was to become standard before returning to Martlesham for further trials. (Via Jet Age Museum)

Gamecock prototype J7497 at Martlesham with the new-style fin and rudder. (Via Phil Butler)

and the new machine was renamed the Gamecock. Sources differ on the number of the contract for the first prototype, either no. 504577 or 506577/24.

Design and construction of J7497 was said to have been completed in less than six months and it first flew in February 1925 with a Bristol Jupiter IV engine of 398 hp (296.9 kW) with open exhausts. It still had the SE5-style fin and rudder of the Grebe but the twin Vickers machine guns were moved down to either side of the pilot with all but their barrels faired in by a new, more rounded fuselage. The basic fuselage frame of the Grebe was virtually unchanged and was essentially that of the Nighthawk.

It was delivered to Martlesham on 20 February but was soon back at the company for a new, enlarged fin and rudder to improve directional stability. It returned to Martlesham on 8 April, then went to Bristol and back again to Brockworth. The first mention in Flight magazine was in the issue of 25 June with a photograph of J7497 at Martlesham and the announcement that it would take part in the fly past at the RAF Display ("*formerly known as the Aerial Pageant*") at Hendon "*on Saturday next*".

J7497 went to Farnborough on 17 August and again on 11 January 1926. It crashed on landing at Farnborough on 3 March.

Second and third prototypes

The second and third prototypes, J7756 and J7757, were ordered on contract no. 571417/25 and it was the second prototype which took part in the RAF Display on 27 June bearing the large black number 1. It was soon off to Martlesham for performance trials on 29 June and went to Farnborough in September. It was back at Brockworth on 23 August 1927 and is last recorded undergoing engine trials with Bristol at Filton.

The third prototype, J7757 was fitted with the more powerful Jupiter VI engine of 425 hp (317 kW). It went to Martlesham in September 1925 for performance trials and to Farnborough on 11 March the following year. It last flew on 19 December 1927.

J7756 was the second Gamecock prototype. Carrying the New Type number 1, it was inspected by HM King George V at the Hendon display on 27 June 1925 (not 1927, as stated in the caption in a Gloster brochure). (Via Jet Age Museum)

Gamecock third prototype J7757 is seen here at Martlesham, where it was sent for performance testing in September 1925. It went to Farnborough six months later and was last flown on 19 December 1927. (Via JD Oughton)

Two shots of the Gamecock third prototype J7757 at Martlesham. (Via Phil Butler)

Test pilots

Initial flight testing by the company was carried out by their chief test pilot Larry Carter but he was badly injured in the high-speed crash of the Gloster II "Bluebird" at Cranwell on 10 June 1925. He did not fly again and after more than a year's illness died in Cheltenham on 27 September 1926 at the age of 28. The company brought in Maurice Piercey as a contract test pilot until the appointment of Howard Saint from RAE Farnborough as the new chief test pilot in January 1927. Some Gamecock testing was also undertaken by Rex Stocken.

Howard Saint was the best known Gamecock test pilot, remembered in particular for cracking the problem of getting the aircraft out of a spin. The RAE News of February 1965 carried a biographical feature on Saint and wrote that the spinning problem *"was not solved until Mr Saint overheard a pilot talking in a Norfolk public house after he had baled out following a violent spin in a Gamecock. The aircraft righted itself immediately he stepped out of the cockpit and Mr Saint thought he had the answer to the problem. By rigging up handle bars on the top main planes and by tying himself into the cockpit Mr Saint put Gloster's vicious little fighter into a spin. He then forced himself out of the cockpit holding on to the bars on the wing and the aircraft came out of the spin. By placing his body in the slipstream he had caused a disturbance of the airflow sufficiently great to right the aircraft. The secret of how it was done remained Mr Saint's for a long time. Once he astounded experts by spinning a Gamecock 34 turns and then pulling out at 200 feet."*

Construction

The Gamecock was to be the RAF's last wooden fighter. The basic wire-braced fuselage consisted of four steam-bent ash longerons with multiple frames and spruce struts. Thinner ply sub-frames and stringers completed the rounded cross section which was clad with metal panels to the front and with fabric covering to the rear. A complex feature was the tailplane incidence adjusting gear, consisting of a pair of vertical jacks with precisely-machined triple-start threads. The engine was bolted to a steel front bulkhead and the second frame incorporated an asbestos firewall. Like the Grebe, the Gamecock used Folland and Preston's patented HLB wing combination with spruce spars, ribs and struts and their patented rubber and oleo undercarriage. The wings were slightly larger than the Grebe's and the underwing fuel tanks were of revised, slimmer design.

Trenchard decides

Air Chief Marshal Sir Hugh Trenchard GCB DSO, known as the "father of the Royal Air Force", was Chief of Air Staff at the Air Ministry while the Gamecock was being assessed at Martlesham and by 56 Squadron. In a memo of 27 April 1925 he wrote: *"On looking at the preliminary report of Martlesham on the Gamecock, I see that the engine is described as 'Jupiter experimental'. ... I am given to understand that this engine has never been type-tested and will not be in production until July at the earliest. I also hear rumours that type-testing may take another three or four months. Does this mean that, if I decide to order Gamecocks for one or two squadrons next week, they will be held up for want of a properly tested engine? ... I must also know by what dates deliveries of Gamecocks could begin, if I accepted the machine next week, and at what rate they would come forward. [Also] how the answer to this last question affects Nos. 23 and 43 Squadrons, of which I specially deferred the formation so that they could have these machines, and No. 17 Squadron, which still has Snipes."*

Sqn Ldr C Portal - later to be just as distinguished, as Lord Portal of Hungerford - replied on 7 May that there were differing assessments of when the Jupiter V would be ready. *"The Gamecock with Jupiter IV will have a considerably worse performance than the present one (probably no better than the Jaguar Grebe). Nos. 23 and 43 Squadrons will have to form with Snipes in any case. In view of the above points I recommend that if you decide to order Gamecocks you should let them wait for the Jupiter V engine".* Four days later Trenchard wrote: *"I saw the Gamecock at Biggin Hill on May 8th. Although the performance is not what I had hoped to get with the Jupiter V engine, the machine shows enough improvement over the Grebe to enable me to accept it as a service type. Its chief advantage over the Grebe is in the position of the guns and in the comfort of the cockpit, due to better screening".* He said that he Gamecock *"will be accepted as a service type"* after certain modifications had been made, in particular *"some form of exhaust ring is required to eliminate exhaust flash for night flying".* Discussions followed about strengthening the Gamecock and the weight penalty this would impose.

Trenchard wrote again on 4 June 1925: *"I cannot agree to the strengthening of this machine, as this will add weight and cause a loss of performance, and I am not satisfied that it is necessary. I would prefer to take the machine as it is, since it is practically certain that this machine will seldom be required in war, and never in peace, to carry all the military load for which provision is made. ... It is essential that the machine is turned out as asked for without the strengthening. ..."*

Into production

Thirty Gloucestershire Gamecock Mk Is were ordered accordingly to specification 18/25, on contract no. 606962/25 dated September of that year. The serial range of this first production batch was J7891 to J7920 and all but two of them went to 23 and 43 Squadrons. A further sixty Gamecocks were ordered for the RAF in three more batches: J8033 to J8047, J8069 to J8095 and J8405 to J8422. Three more squadrons operated the Gamecock, nos. 3, 17 and 32. All were fitted with the Jupiter VI of 425 hp (317 kW).

Gamecock squadrons

In spite of Trenchard's intentions, when 23 and 43 Squadrons were reformed on 1 July 1925 they had to operate the almost-obsolete Sopwith Snipe as interim equipment. It was not until April 1926 that they were able to take delivery of their Gamecocks.

23 Squadron

With its distinctive markings of red and blue squares, 23 Squadron was the most photographed of all the RAF's Gamecock units. It would also operate the Gamecock for considerably longer than any other squadron, for about five and a half years. Douglas Bader of 23 Squadron is the best-known Gamecock pilot nowadays but at the time the squadron's best-known personality was Raymond Collishaw, the WW1 Sopwith Triplane ace. The much-decorated airman, with the DSO, OBE, DSC and DFC, was 23's Squadron Commander from 1 July 1925 until November 1927. His successors were Sqn Ldr AG Jones-Williams MC from January 1928 to December 1929 and Sqn Ldr HH Woollett DSO MC from January 1930 to December 1931.

Gamecocks of 23 Squadron taxi past the camera. J7892 served with the squadron from May 1926 to April 1928. Note the central bomb carrier and the seatbelt anchoring points aft of the radio compartment. (Author's collection)

Two unidentified Gamecocks of "A" Flight, 23 Squadron, at Kenley - believed to be taken in 1927. (Author's collection)

The officers and men of A Flight, 23 (Fighter) Squadron pose in front of one of their Gamecocks at RAF Kenley in December 1927. The aircraft has the extra centre section struts but not the extra outer wing struts. Front row, left to right: LAC E Athey, A/C2 M Haworth, A/C1 C Baker, F/O GS Gardiner, Flt Lt J MacG Fairweather DFC [Flight Commander], P/O HA Purvis, LAC W Pine, A/C1 J Hendry and LAC H Hasthorpe. Back row, left to right: A/C1 WAC "Billie" Cooper, A/C1 SE Hammond, A/C1 J Dixon, Sgt HA Duncton, Sgt J Treadwell, Flight Sgt FC Lewis, A/C1 GH Baldock, A/C1 F Chard, Cpl G Wyborn and LAC HG Winton. (From Rob Cooper, son of William Cooper, via Jet Age Museum)

J7904, which served with 23 squadron between July 1929 and November 1930, photographed at Sealand, probably in 1930, with outer vee interplane struts fitted. It was previously on the strength of 43 Squadron, between March 1926 and May 1927, where it was the Squadron Commander's mount, as represented by Jet Age Museum's Gamecock reproduction. (Via John Adams)

Refuelling Gamecock J7896, which was with 23 Squadron between May 1926 and January 1929. (Via Jet Age Museum)

J8092 of 23 Squadron with chequers on the fuselage spine, outer vee interplane struts and a camera gun on the lower starboard wing. (Via Jet Age Museum)

J8092 served with 23 Squadron from August 1928. It was damaged in collision with Vickers Virginia bomber J7567 on 8 March 1929 but was repaired and remained with the squadron until May 1930. (Via Jet Age Museum)

The squadron was initially based at RAF Henlow, moving to RAF Kenley on 6 February 1927. It remained there until late 1932, although in September 1931 the Gamecocks were replaced by Bulldogs.

Douglas Bader and the Gamecock, 1931

As a young 23 Squadron Pilot Officer - he joined in August 1930 - the famous legless World War II fighter ace Douglas Bader was renowned for his aerobatic display in the Gamecock with his fellow pilot Flight Lieutenant Harry Day. The Times of 29 June 1931 reported record attendance at the annual RAF Display at Hendon: *"At least 175,000 people were inside the aerodrome, and crowded hillsides, fields and streets to the north, west and south were so filled with people that hundreds of thousands probably watched the performance from outside. ... As an example of pure skill in piloting the event of the day was the aerobatic display by Flight Lieutenant HM Day and Pilot Officer DRS Bader of No. 23 Squadron. They were flying the finest aerobatic machines in the world, Gloster Gamecocks, which in four successive years have been chosen for this type of work at the display. On Saturday the work was done with a steadiness and perfection in timing which accounted for the advice of officers who had seen rehearsals that their friends should not seek the tea tent until this exhibition was over. The two machines looped and rolled alongside each other. They dived towards each other, zoomed until they could climb no more, and then made stalled turns together. They spun upwards on parallel courses and then made downward spins. Their exhibition lasted 10 minutes and was full of the cleanest trick flying, synchronised to a fraction of a second."*

The twelve Gamecocks of 23 Squadron lined up at RAF Kenley in 1927. J8084, nearest the camera, was the Gamecock of the Squadron Commander, the renowned WW1 ace Squadron Leader Raymond Collishaw DSO OBE DSC DFC. The second and third machines from the camera are J8040 and J7907. Douglas Bader is among the pilots in the line-up. (From Rob Cooper, son of A/C1 William Cooper, standing in front of the starboard wing of the second aircraft, via Jet Age Museum)

As a young Flying Officer the famous legless World War II fighter ace Douglas Bader of 23 Squadron (right in photo) was renowned for his aerobatic display in the Gamecock with his fellow pilot Flight Lieutenant Harry Day. (Author's collection)

Flight's report of the display described how the two Gamecocks mirrored each other: "*[W]hen the two machines approached each other in a roll or some other manoeuvre, the distance between them was small enough to maintain the illusion of the mirror, at least until the two machines met and 'passed through the looking glass'. ... Altogether the demonstration was very pretty*". Day's Gamecock was J7914 but the identity of Bader's is not known. It was after 23 Squadron changed over to Bristol Bulldogs that Bader lost his legs when he touched the ground and crashed during a low-level slow roll.

43 Squadron

Famous as the Fighting Cocks and adopting a picture of a (feathered) gamecock as the squadron badge, 43 vies with 23 Squadron as the first to be equipped with the new fighter. It was re-formed on 1 July 1925 and, like 23, it received its Gamecocks in April 1926, replacing Sopwith Snipes. It parted with them in April 1928, a full three and a half years earlier than its rival. John Rawlings wrote that the Gamecocks "*formed the foundation for No 43 aerobatic prowess, a prowess which came to its height with Hawker Furies in the thirties*".

With their distinctive black and white chequers, 43's Gamecocks were based at Henlow until December 1926, when the squadron moved to Tangmere. The CO was Sqn Ldr AF Brooke, appointed in July 1926 at the same time as Collishaw to 23 Squadron; he commanded until 10 January 1928 when he was succeeded by Sqn Ldr CN Lowe MC DFC. A total of 26 Gamecocks saw service with the squadron. Three of them crashed in squadron service, all in the Tangmere area: J7919 at North Marsden, near Emsworth; J8418

A rare air-to-air photograph of a Gamecock: J8037 was on the strength of 43 Squadron from October 1926 to August 1927. (Via Jet Age Museum)

Three Gamecocks of 43 Squadron in flight formation over Hamble airfield on 31 May 1928 when they per-
formed at the Hampshire Air Pageant. The flight commander's Gamecock, J8090, has a streamer and a pointed
spinner. It served with the squadron between October 1927 and June 1928. J7908, nearest the camera, was
with the squadron between April 1926 and June 1928. The third aircraft, J8415, was one of the last Gamecocks
to be built and served with the squadron between October 1927 and June 1928. It was then transferred to 23
Squadron, but was written off after colliding with Gamecock J8094 1,800 feet (549 m) above RAF Kenley. (Via
JD Oughton)

Another 43 Squadron Gamecock, J7918. It was with the squadron
from April 1926 to July 1927. (Via Jet Age Museum)

into woods on Trundle Hill at Eastergate, near Chichester; and J8420, which failed to recover from a spin. An ex-43 Squadron Gamecock, J7906, crashed when being tested from the Gloster airfield (see Junor's crash, below).

Sqn Ldr Brooke, known as "Pongo", worked wonders transforming 43 into an elite squadron. He joined the Royal Flying Corps from a crack cavalry regiment, the 10th Hussars, in 1915. Wounded in 1918 soon after the formation of the new Royal Air Force, he was awarded a permanent commission in 1920. He served with 27 Squadron in India, at the RAF Depot (Inland Area), with the Boys' Wing at Cranwell, at the Air Ministry and with 17 Squadron at Hawkinge before becoming 43's CO. His personal Gamecock, J7904, wore a tapering stripe of black and white chequers along the rear fuselage spine in addition to the usual squadron markings. Posted to 28 Squadron in India when he left the squadron, he returned to the RAF Depot at Uxbridge in September 1931 and just over a year later retired due to ill health.

The squadron was also known as "Kate Meyrick's Own" after the nightclub owner Mrs Meyrick who ran the fashionable Forty-Three Club in London's Gerrard Street at the time. She has been called *"the most notorious night club owner and the most gaoled woman in London"*.

32 Squadron

The third squadron to be equipped with Gamecocks was 32 Squadron at Kenley which received its new fighters in September 1926. Sqn Ldr RB Mansell had taken over as CO the previous month. This was the only squadron to operate both the Grebe and the Gamecock. Both types carried the squadron's blue band with diagonal breaks. The Siskin IIIA replaced the Gamecock in June 1928.

32 Squadron at Kenley operated the Gamecock for less than two years, from September 1926 to June 1928, and was the only squadron equipped with both Grebe and Gamecock. The aircraft on the right is J8043 with what look like flight commander's colours on the tailplane. It was among the squadron's first Gamecocks, surviving until 16 May 1927 when it collided in formation with J8043. J8072, on the left, is not recorded as serving with 32 Squadron at all, although the markings here are clear enough - it is only listed by Air Britain as serving with the Armament & Gunnery School. (Author's collection)

17 Squadron

Based at Upavon during the Gamecock period, 3 and 17 were sister squadrons which had specialised in night fighting since 1925, equipped with Hawker Woodcocks. 17 Squadron received its Gamecocks first, in January 1928, and only operated the type until September, when they were superseded by Armstrong Whitworth Siskins. Only three Gamecock serials are recorded for 17 Squadron. The aircraft were marked with the squadron's distinctive double black zigzag. J8408 was the squadron commander's aircraft, painted with striking orange fin, tailplane and upper rear fuselage (there is excellent artwork by Peter Endsleigh Castle ARAeS of this machine in the Gamecock Profile). It's not clear which squadron commander this was, though. Sqn Ldr J Leacroft MC led the squadron from April 1924 until April 1928, when he was succeeded by Sqn Ldr AR Arnold DSO DFC.

Photographs of 3 Squadron Gamecocks are rare and only 12 are recorded as serving with the squadron. No serial is visible but note the broad coloured band on the lower port wing. (Author's collection)

3 Squadron

After a Woodcock accident in August 1928 the type was withdrawn and 3 Squadron at Upavon received its Gamecocks in the same month, operating the type until June the following year when they in turn were replaced by Bristol Bulldogs. Throughout the Gamecock's service the squadron was led by Sqn Ldr E Digby Johnson AFC, who took over the squadron in September 1927 and stayed until August 1930. The squadron markings were a single bright green bar.

19 Squadron

Only one Gamecock is recorded as serving with this squadron, J8035. This was a former 43 Squadron machine which had served with the Fighting Cocks from August 1926 until June 1928, so its spell with 19 Squadron must have been at Duxford alongside their standard equipment at the time of the Siskin IIIA (March 1928 to September 1931). It carried the squadron's blue and white check markings.

Gamecock J7895, the fifth production aircraft, photographed at Brockworth before it was delivered to 23 Squadron in May 1926. It served with the squadron until November 1928. (Author's collection)

This close up view of J7895's tail clearly shows the stencil markings, rear fuselage stitching and seatbelt attachment points. (Author's collection)

J8033, the first Gamecock of the second production batch, photographed at Brockworth. It must have been built in 1926 but no service is recorded until it went to the Armament & Gunnery School from April 1928 to October 1930. (Author's collection)

J8033 at Brockworth again, without machine guns fitted. The building in the background was the golf club. (Author's collection)

A company photograph of an early production Gamecock on the grass at Brockworth. (Jet Age Museum/Russell Adams Collection)

The same photograph was used in this company advertisement of 1926, with some artistic licence taken with the rigging wires. (Via Jet Age Museum)

What the well-dressed Gamecock pilot was wearing, from the 1927 Wonder Book of Aircraft. (Author's collection)

"GLOSTER"

Telegrams:
'OLOSAIRCRA' CHELTENHAM
'OLOSAIRCRA' WESTCENT LONDON

Telephones:
Nº 1161-2-3-4 CHELTENHAM
Nº 3655 MUSEUM LONDON

THE GLOUCESTERSHIRE AIRCRAFT Co. Ltd.

SUNNINGEND WORKS
CHELTENHAM

London Office : 49, RATHBONE PLACE, W.1

DESIGNERS & MAKERS
OF ALL
TYPES OF AIRCRAFT

for British and Foreign Governments.

Gamecock with Jupiter Engine.

WINNERS OF THE AERIAL DERBY, 1921—2—3

RECORD CLIMB OF 19,500-ft. in 11 mins. 34 secs.
WITH GLOSTER-NAPIER I.

Enquiries invited.   *Illustrated catalogue on application.*

[R.A.F. Official—Crown Copyright.]
A HIGH-FLYING PILOT.
He is equipped with wireless telephone, oxygen-breathing apparatus, heated clothing, and parachute.

LEADS TO
Goggles
Oxygen
Microphone
Heated clothing
Telephones

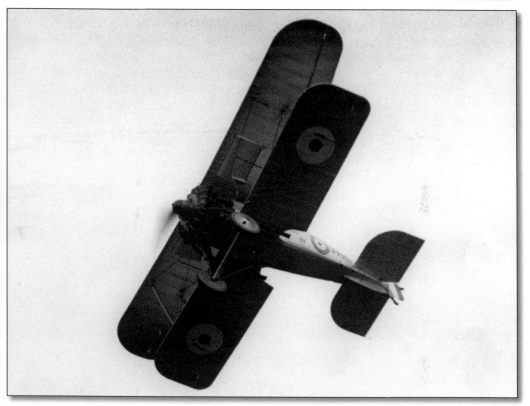

Gamecock J7910 was briefly with 23 Squadron before returning to Gloster, then went to Martlesham - see next two pictures. (Via JD Oughton)

J7910 photographed at Martlesham, where it went for dive and anti-flutter trials between May and July 1927. It is now fitted with no less than eight extra struts in an attempt to cure the wing flutter problem: four sprouting from the fuselage and four more outboard of the interplane struts. (Via JD Oughton)

Side view of Gamecock J7910. (Via Phil Butler)

Gamecock J8089 served with the Central Flying School at Digby between December 1928 and April 1929 and later with 23 Squadron and No. 3 Flying Training School. It swung and crashed taking off at Spitalgate on 25 March 1931. (Via JD Oughton)

The only dual control Gamecock: J7900 served as a single seater with 43 Squadron between March and June1926 before being converted by Gloster and going to Central Flying School in October 1927. (Via JD Oughton)

A mixed formation of Central Flying School aircraft in 1931, with Gamecock J8076 on the left. It had previously been with 23 Squadron and No. 2 Flying Training School. The other aircraft, going away from the camera, are Atlas K1471, Moth K1214, Fairey IIIF K1160, Avro 504N ?K1603, Siskin J9322 and an unidentified Bulldog. (Author's collection)

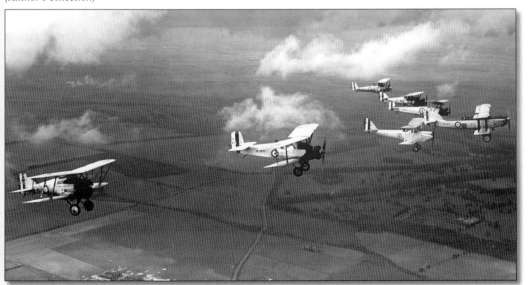

Other RAF service

Apart from the various Gamecocks which went to Martlesham, seven were on the strength of Central Flying School at various times, one of them (J7900) the only recorded dual-control Gamecock. One was on the books of the RAF College at Cranwell, four spent time at the Armament & Gunnery School, one served with each of Nos 2 and 3 Flying Training School and five with Home Communications Flight. Serials are listed at the end of the Gamecock section.

Horniman's display, 1928

A spectacular display of aerobatics was given by Flt Lt RH Horniman of Headquarters, RAF Kenley, in the 1928 Royal Air Force Display at Hendon. Flight magazine described the *"wings of scarlet which flashed so effectively against the deep blue sky"*. A photo of Horniman's Gamecock inverted over Hendon featured in a Gloster advertisement soon afterwards and it's clear that the underside was still in the standard service silver finish, so we must assume that only the upper surfaces were scarlet. Flight also cast light on the fighting tactics of the day: *"The most thrilling item in the plane's exhibition was the 'rocket'. Approaching the enclosures at a low height, he suddenly shot upwards in a swift, straight, and almost vertical climb and continued until he must have been nearly 2,000 ft high. This movement is useful for a single-seater machine when engaging an enemy bomber, for it can fire underneath in a position almost immune from the bomber's return fire."*

Junor's crash

Several Gamecocks were lost in crashes, mostly due to wing flutter or to the difficulty of getting out of a spin. One such crash took place on 19 August 1926 when RAE test pilot Flt Lt HR Junor DFC was flying from Gloster's Brockworth airfield to investigate flutter. Gamecock J7906, a 43 Squadron machine, was back at the factory and Junor was killed when the ailerons detached and the machine broke up in the air.

Gloster inspector Basil Fielding described the incident in detail in his unpublished memoirs:

"This story concerns the testing of the Gamecock aircraft. Maurice Piercey did most of this for the GAC at Brockworth. In the early stages he met with considerable aileron flutter, several times after dives at approx. 300 miles per hour he used to land with knuckles on both hands bleeding. He told me it was most violent and the only way he could get it out of a dive was to put both arms round the control column, clasp his fingers together and gradually ease the stick back with the control column going from side to side faster than he could count. The trouble was investigated and it was thought it was caused by the length of top spar between centre section struts and outer wing struts and the overhang between wing struts and wing tips which caused bad flexing. To cure the trouble additional struts were fitted from the bottom of the centre section struts to a point on the top spar about three feet out. This reduced the distance between points of support. It was then flown again by Piercey and the trouble appeared cured. It was then decided to get several service pilots to fly it before sending the aircraft to the RAF. I believe it was a Flt Lt King from Martlesham that flew it next, and he was unable to obtain flutter. Then came another Flt Lt from a Service Squadron, his name I can't remember, he could not obtain flutter.
Lastly came Flt Lt Junor from RAE Farnborough. He flew up and said he was anxious to get back as soon as possible. Apart from [Cyril] Lisney [the AID inspector], myself and a few mechanics no one else was at the drome. I handed him his clearance chit for flight and he remarked "Is it necessary for me to carry this?" I replied "The

instructions lay down that one must be handed to the pilot". He jokingly remarked "OK I'll take it, I suppose it must be found on the body". These words will always remain in my memory. He took off and flew towards Cheltenham, climbing steeply, then put the nose down in the direction of Churchdown. Lisney and I stood on the drome watching him. Suddenly we saw pieces falling away and the aircraft coming down, out of control. We jumped in the old Ford and dashed off down the Brockworth Road. Before reaching the Wagon and Horses we saw flames in a garden opposite. I pulled the car into the hedge, stood on the door and jumped out. A few yards away was the parachute, fully opened and the pilot underneath, face downwards. We lifted him over, but could find no sign of life. Looking up we heard shouting, the aircraft was standing on end, flames reaching several feet high. ... This meant further modifications, one I believe was the fitting of wires from bottom of wing struts to wing tips. The trouble was eventually cured and the aircraft went into production and proved a good machine."

Wheatley's crash

Flt Lt G Wheatley, an A&AEE test pilot, was killed on 8 December 1926 at Martlesham when his Gamecock J7891 broke up near the airfield some ten minutes after take off. The ailerons had been balanced as part of the ongoing programme of attempts to cure the Gamecock's wing flutter.

Gloster chargehand "Nobby" Clarke standing by the new Hele-Shaw Beacham VP propeller fitted to an unarmed Gamecock at Brockworth. (Via Jet Age Museum)

VP propeller Gamecock

Development was also being carried out with aircraft still on service charge. J8075, an otherwise standard late production Gamecock I, was used in 1929 on further trials of the Hele-Shaw Beacham variable pitch propeller, which in this case involved the use of a very large louvred spinner.

J8075 photographed in February 1927 during VP propeller trials, unarmed and with a huge ventilated spinner and a full set of extra wing struts. It was used as a development aircraft, also testing the 450 hp (336 kW) Bristol Mercury Mk IIA and being converted to Gamecock II standard. (Author's collection)

Gamecock II

Early in 1928 the wraps were taken off the first Gamecock II. It was the only Mk II to look like the RAF Gamecock as it was built in the hope of an order for the RAF and still used the prominent frontal exhaust manifold system of the Mk I. Viewed from below in the air it could be seen to have new wings with the semi-circular tips and long parallel narrow-chord ailerons which had been tried out on J7910.

Although using the old wing structure as a basis, the new wings and their assembly were changed to a completely new format. The inboard sections of the old "centre-line joined" mainplanes over the width of the trailing edge cutaway were done away with and replaced by an orthodox centre section of the same width with its own cutaway. The adjacent sections of the mainplanes remained in the same place as did the fuel tanks and their feeds, although the fuel tanks had been redesigned with a shallower curve on the underside so that they projected less below the bottom wing surface and interfered less with the airflow. The interplane struts now sloped outwards, the tops having been moved outwards one rib space, no doubt with flutter problems in mind to shorten the top wing overhang and improve stiffness.

The new centre section had steel tubes across the width connecting the mainplane spars, and as the trailing edge cutout reduced the chord at this point, maintaining the same form of aerofoil section reduced the thickness and allowed the lower surface to be raised to give an improved forward view. The greatest improvement in view,

Gamecock II prototype J8804 was fitted with a 425 hp (317 kW) Jupiter VIA. It was tested at both Martlesham and Farnborough at various dates between June 1927 and January 1929 and was fitted for a time with the enlarged rudder seen here. (Via JD Oughton)

After dive and anti-flutter trials at Martlesham as a Gamecock I (see above), J7910 was coverted to Gamecock II standard and photographed between Nos. 2 and 3 Hangars at Brockworth. The civil Grebe G-EBHA can be glimpsed in No. 2 Hangar behind. (Author's collection)

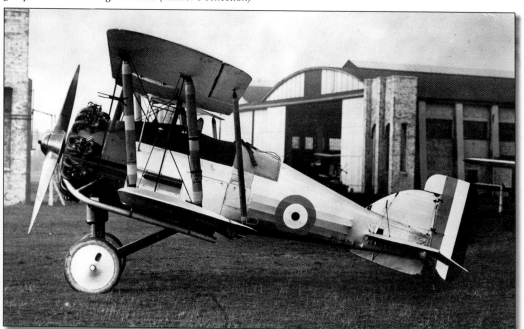

J7910 converted to Gamecock II standard. (Author's collection)

The unmarked Gamecock II J7910 flies low over Brockworth airfield for the Flight cameraman, piloted by Howard Saint. (Flight, from author's collection)

however, was brought about because the central pyramid supporting struts of the Mk I were now replaced by two struts at each side of the centre section, each pair being braced by a diagonal strut between the top of the left hand strut and the bottom of the right hand strut.

It is sometimes difficult to appreciate how so many designers failed to consider the pilot's view from the cockpit to be a foremost consideration. In early "boxkite" aeroplanes the pilot's view was invariably very good, but when, in the first world war, the tractor biplane proved to be the most efficient layout, there was nowhere to put the pilot but at the back behind the wings, where his view of where he was going and what was ahead of him was atrocious. This set a pattern which undoubtedly had a bad effect on designers' standards, and the centre-line strutting of the Grebe/Gamecock I top wing attachment showed that at the time the structural convenience outweighed any consideration of pilot's view, even on a fighter. Although the HLB format was trialled on the Grouse, the centreline upper wing join supported by inverted vee struts was that of the Bamel - the difference being that the Bamel's wingspan was so small that flutter was not an issue, as it became on the Grebe and Gamecock.

The basic reason for introducing the centre section on the Gamecock II was increased structural rigidity as an anti-flutter measure, and one might have thought that the improvement in the pilot's view had no part in the change were it not for the fact that the lower surface formed an arch providing a bigger gap above the fuselage. This, like the cockpit entry flap, showed that Henry Folland was taking some notice of pilot's comments, a relatively new idea in spite of the employment of experienced professional test pilots. The "clear view Grebe" experiments would have played their part in this change as well.

The prototype II was given a great deal of publicity and many photographs were published, including a number of flight views taken on a press visit in 1927 when it was flown by Howard Saint to good effect on low level runs past the camera. The photos were not published in Flight until 27 September 1928, when they were described as being taken "some little time ago". Produced as a private venture, it had no service serial number although the fuselage with its engine, tail unit and undercarriage must have been taken from a service Gamecock I, as evidenced by the RAF navigation light bracket still in place on the rudder. No serial number appears on the stencil markings either.

In 1928 it was purchased for testing by the RAF and became J8804, by which time it had acquired a rudder whose area was increased by curving the trailing edge. It could be said that this looked prettier than its angular predecessor but nobody seems to have accepted responsibility for it and this mod disappeared without trace.

Gamecock "III"

In the meantime Glosters had continued Gamecock development with another airframe, J8047. After RAF service this machine had been used at RAE Farnborough for spinning trials which led to the wings being moved back about four inches (100 mm). Returned to Glosters on experimental contract it retained the old wings joined on the centre line but modified to have long narrow-chord ailerons and round wing tips like those tried out on J7910.

It retained the RAF-style frontal exhaust manifold but the fuselage was lengthened by 22 inches (just under 560 mm) to 21 ft 6 in (6.55 m). The undercarriage had the track widened by a foot (305 mm) to six feet (1.83 m) and the shock absorber leg attachment was moved back from the base of the No. 1 (engine) bulkhead to the No. 2 (fireproof) bulkhead, making the leg almost vertical in the flight position. The tail was also changed to add about eight inches (200 mm) to the height, providing a taller rudder and fin and increasing their areas. A small triangular tip was added to the top of the fin to fill in the step in outline that was a prominent feature of all other Gamecocks. A reference made to an increase in tailplane area does not show up on photographs and it is thought that this was probably due to the fairly common error of referring to the fin and rudder as the "tailplane".

Stretched Gamecock: J8047 began life in 1926 as a standard Mk I, first at Central Flying School and then under-taking spinning trials at Farnborough. Heavily modified by Gloster, it made its first flight as the so-called "Mk III" on 25 June 1928 at Brockworth, where these photographs were taken. A 450 hp (336 kW) Jupiter VII was fitted in March 1928 and a Hele-Shaw Beacham VP propeller three months later. The original Jupiter VI was re-fitted in 1932, the tailplane was enlarged and it went back to Farnborough for further spinning trials. It was sold off in 1934, becoming G-ADIN. (Author's collection)

Gamecock "III" J8047 and VP propeller

Having proved the new fuselage, undercarriage, tail and wing position, J8047 then continued in use for further development, carrying out trials fitted with a supercharged Jupiter VII and additional trials with the Hele-Shaw Beacham variable pitch propeller.

At Glosters it was said at this time to be called, unofficially, the Mk III, which of course was a misconception as it was not as up-to-date as the production Mk II was to become, still having a modified form of the old centre-line-joined wing. However it was quite understandable as it bristled with updated changes and except for the wing centre section most of the later modifications had been tried out on it, plus others which were not adopted in production aircraft.

Gamecocks for Finland

In spite of good reports in RAF trials of J8804 an order was not placed for the Gamecock II, leaving Glosters without a customer. Providentially, Finland had earlier shown an interest in the Gamecock. The Finnish Air Force had a succession of unsatisfactory fighter types since its formation in 1917. Aware of the performance of the RAF's Grebes and Gamecocks, they approached Gloster and Major V Wuori, head of the Finnish Air Force, visited Brockworth aerodrome in July 1926. He was escorted by Sqn Ldr Field, who was on loan by the British Air Ministry as an adviser to the Finnish Air Force.

Gloster wasted no time in building a second prototype identical to J8804 except for dispensing with the RAF-style frontal exhaust manifold in favour of stub exhausts and fitting a pointed spinner and faired cowling.

Gloster's first Gamecock pattern aircraft for Finland was GA-38, seen here at Brockworth. It was essentially a Gamecock II like J8804 but without the exhaust collector ring. (Via Jack Meaden)

GA-38 in Finland with ski undercarriage fitted. (Author's collection)

It was taken to Finland and demonstrated by Howard Saint in March 1927, making an excellent impression on the Finns. The climax of the Finnish Air Pageant at Helsinki on 25 March - following such attractions as balloon bursting, parachute descents, low-level bombing and "destruction of a village" - was an aerobatic display by Saint. The Gamecock was duly purchased by them as G-38 and fitted with skis on a trial basis, followed by an order for a production version and an agreement for Finnish production under sub-contract. Gloster stated that they "*constructed and delivered their machine in the short space of six weeks.*"

G-38 was really a second prototype, and like J8804 the only Mk II features were the wings. The production Mk II pattern aircraft supplied to Finland as G-43 was very different as it married the new wing of the prototypes to a new fuselage, undercarriage and tail unit (except for the fin tip) as developed on J8047. Bays 1-2 and 5-6 were lengthened by a total of 2 ft 2 in (660 mm). All other bays remained the same length as the Gamecock I.

Another shot of GA-38 in Finland. (Via Jack Meaden)

Gloster's second Gamecock pattern aircraft for Finland, GA-43, had the longer fuselage and larger fin and rudder which would be typical of the standard production Kukko. (Via JD Oughton)

If anything was to have been called the Mk III it should have been G-43, as it was the only Gamecock produced by Gloster which had all the new features, but the Finnish Gamecock had been identified as the Mk II initially and it was not practical to allow improvements to affect this.

G-38 was finished in standard silver with dark front fuselage panels and top decking. Photographed at Brockworth airfield before delivery, Gloster's artistic interpretation of Finnish markings is noticeable: the swastikas on port and starboard wings are handed, incorrectly - and in opposite directions on the upper and lower surfaces. The later G-43 had the same error.

Finnish production, using G-43 as the pattern aircraft, consisted of 15 fighters spread over two years to 1930 and numbered G-44 to G-58. They could have skis substituted for the wheels, as tried out on G-38, and on some advantage was taken of the side-entry cockpit door to fit streamlined head fairings on the fuselage behind the cockpit.

GA-43 in flight. (Via Jack Meaden)

Their engines were Gnome-Rhone licence-built Jupiter IV, initially IVA 9Ab and 9Ak of 420 hp (313 kW) and later IV 9Ag of 480 hp (358 kW). The Gloster-built prototypes did not have navigation lights when supplied but the Finnish-built aircraft had them built into the top wing leading edge tip and the rudder trailing edge. The Finns called them *Kukko* (Cock, not Cuckoo as some sources state).

At the time of the 1939-40 Winter War nine Kukkos were still in service as fighter trainers with the central flying school at Kauhava and with T-LLv 29 and 34 conversion squadrons. They had finally been taken out of front-line service with HLeLv 24 at Immola, replaced by 36 Fokker D.XXIs. One of them was credited with the capture on 29 January 1940 of a Soviet Ilyushin DB-3M bomber by preventing its crew from setting fire to it after it landed on the frozen Lake Roinevesi at Hauho because lack of fuel. Other DBs landed to help the downed bomber, but they were strafed by W/O Jääskeläinen of T-LLv 29, forcing them to take off again. The captured aircraft later served with the Finnish Air Force.

GA-38 was scrapped on 11 October 1941 after logging 937 flying hours. The last serving Finnish Gamecock II was G-46, finally scrapped after a landing accident in July 1944. A rear fuselage displayed in the Finnish Aviation Museum is of the last Finnish-built Gamecock Mk II GA-58 (production number 15). It was delivered on 15 May 1930 and remained in service until it crashed on 10 March 1940, killing its pilot. It had logged a total of 688 hours 35 minutes.

✳   ✳   ✳

Gloster chief inspector Basil Fielding went to Finland to supervise production in the early stages. He wrote an account of the trip in his unpublished memoirs. *"Referring to the Finnish Government buying 2 Gamecocks and a set of drawings it was not long after that they ran into trouble. The first thing they did (or our company did) was to convert the English Dimensions to the Metric equivalents or as near as possible and when it came to matching parts most were half a mil up or half a mil down. Trouble was also experienced in obtaining steel to the specifica-*

Gamecock reproduction chief designer Roff Jones noted: "I think this airframe is one of the first four Kukkos built in the Finnish National Aircraft Factory Helsinki in 1929. ... The bay 1-2 is the one which has been lengthened and the bay 5-6 was also lengthened; all other bays are the same length as Gamecock I." (Via Jet Age Museum)

Production Kukko GA-52 fitted with skis. The wheeled and ski undercarriages were interchangeable. (Author's collection)

A production Kukko with dark green upper and light blue undersurfaces. The wing tips and probably the spinner were yellow. (Via JD Oughton)

tions called up as most of this had to be obtained from England and there were long delays. Eventually they asked GAC for help and the late Wally Vick of the DO and the writer were instructed to go out and help clear up the job.

"... The small aircraft factory was situated on an island about 4 miles from Helsinki. We were told it was originally an old Russian fort, the walls were at least 4-5 feet thick. We went by tug and returned each day and had our midday meal there. ... Vick's job consisted of going through all the drawings and clearing up the dimensions on matching parts, and most of his work was done in conjunction with the Chief Designer. My job consisted on inspecting parts already produced and deciding what I considered acceptable and scrapping parts made which were unserviceable.

Three Finnish Air Force Kukko pilots - and a good view of the cockpit entrance door and three-piece windscreen. (Via Jet Age Museum)

"... Numerous queries were discussed and settled but two remained vividly in my mind. I found a number of fuel tanks with a round hole about a foot in diameter cut in the top. I enquired why they had done this and he replied 'but your tanks in the machines have one also and a dome is riveted on the top'. Then I remembered, after our tanks were fitted the Finns asked for extra tankage and to give them this we had to resort to this procedure. The drawings supplied to the Finns gave the tankage required without doing this, so plates were made up and the tanks sealed again.

"Another trouble I found was that the tubing supplied for part of the rear fuselage was two gauges down so I rejected it. But they informed me it would hold the job up as it would take at least six months to get supplies of the correct gauge tubing, so the matter was taken up with their Drawing Office. We got over this trouble by filling each tube with a spruce plug which gave the the the necessary strength factor. The extra weight affected the CG very little and you could tell no difference in the job once assembled."

Gamecocks for Sweden

An unidentified source in the company's publicity files states that *"a special Mk II version was evolved for the Swedish Air Force powered by a French Gnome et Rhone Jupiter IV"*. I have not found anything else to corroborate this.

Civil Gamecocks

While RAF squadrons were equipped with the Gamecock, Glosters had their own civil registered Gamecock, G-EBNT, for a year. It was registered on 17 March 1926 and transferred to the RAF as J8033 in March 1927 (the civil registration was cancelled on 27 April). In place of the frontal exhaust manifold assembly of the service version it had stub exhausts, a pointed spinner and circular fairing, giving it a more streamlined appearance. In addition it had smaller wheels and tyres and slightly longer undercarriage legs giving better propeller ground clearance.

After eight years of service Gamecock "III" J8047 was taken off Air Ministry charge and put up for sale. It was bought by JW "Bill" Tomkins, overhauled, fitted with a Jupiter VIIFP and registered G-ADIN on 3 June

Two fine shots of Gloster's civil demonstrator Gamecock G-EBNT. Note the prominent airfield name on the hangar roof. (Flight photographs, from author's collection)

The unarmed Gamecock civil demonstrator G-EBNT was given its Certificate of Airworthiness on 26 March 1926. It lacked the distinctive exhaust collector ring of the RAF version. The original rounded spinner soon gave way to a more pointed one. (Via Jack Meaden, above and author's collection, below)

Another shot of G-EBNT. (Author's collection)

G-ADIN was not the only privately-owned Gamecock (see text) but it was the only one to fly. Bought by farmer JW Tomkins in 1934, it was rebuilt with a 490 hp (366 kW) Jupiter VIIFP and flown by him from September 1935 until it was written off in May 1936. (Author's collection)

1935. The Air Ministry controlled civil airworthiness in those days, and after inspection they granted C of A No. 5133 valid for six months. It was renewed on expiry but shortly after, in May 1936, the aircraft was written off at Sywell after a heavy landing when the undercarriage collapsed and it overturned.

When it first appeared in its civil markings it was seen to have the ailerons modified to have a mass balances on all four, extending forward below the bottom surface on tubular arms. These were most likely fitted during anti-flutter experiments at the time of the later trials carried out when the aircraft was J8047, as the cost of carrying out such a modification on a civil basis would almost certainly have been prohibitive.

Bill Tomkins was the only private owner to successfully fly a Gamecock, but an ex-service Gamecock I which had previously served with 23 Squadron, J8420, was purchased and modified by Reginald Reid of Leith in 1933. By February 1935 it had reached the stage of having what appeared to be a motor car engine and small propeller, and a horizontal steering wheel like that of an omnibus. No wings or tailplane were fitted at this stage and it is unlikely that they ever were, as it was said that "*it could be housed in an ordinary one-car garage*" and it was "*instantly adaptable to road travel*". The only provision for road travel appeared to be a tailwheel in place of the tailskid, but how the "steering wheel" controlled it directionally was not apparent. Although the publicity information issued with it said it was "*intended to provide safe and speedy flying*" its features suggested that the "inventor" knew nothing about flying, and the practical-looking engine mounting and other features suggested that he was an engineer who had modified it as a ground machine just for fun and was pulling everyone's leg about it being intended to fly.

The civil registration G-EBOE was issued on 20 May 1926 for a Gamecock with a 495 hp (369 kW) turbo-supercharged Bristol Orion, a high-altitude Jupiter development with the same bore and stroke but a completely different crankcase and cylinder design. Metallurgical problems meant that the Orion was not flight tested until 1928. The civil registration was cancelled on 19 March that year and the Gamecock was completed with the serial J9248. Flying from Farnborough, it maintained full power to more than 20,000 feet (6096 m), which it reached in less than 13 minutes. It crashed at Bagshot on 9 August 1929.

Flying the Gamecock
by Jack Meaden

Although development was a continuing process and detail improvements in design were taking place all the time, the basic nature of flying was little changed. Flying was still "by the seat of the pants" especially for the fighter boys, whose attention was necessarily directed outside the cockpit most of the time. Flying was very much limited by the weather and poor visibility or storm force winds were common reasons for grounding all aircraft. Airfields were grass areas on which aircraft could start their run from any point on the perimeter necessary to allow them to take off directly into wind. Starting the engine was by hand-swinging the propeller or by Hucks starter, a device designed by early aviation pioneer BC Hucks which was mounted on a small vehicle such as a Model T Ford and had an engine-driven shaft which engaged a claw on the nose of the aircraft's propeller shaft to rotate it for starting.

Chocks had to be placed in front of the wheels before starting and were not pulled away by ground crew until the engine had been warmed at low revs, run up to take-off power and tested on each of its two magnetos. The pilot would then wave the chocks away and taxy out for take off. With no brakes, there was nothing to stop the aircraft weathercocking into wind except the pilot's use of the throttle and rudder and the drag of the tailskid on the ground, so when winds were strong it was often necessary to have a man on each wingtip to assist directional control when taxying. When exercises were being held and orders for interceptions were expected it was usual to line up the "Battle Flight" aircraft on the downwind side of the field with engines ready-warmed and tested.

Parachute straps, already adjusted to the pilot, had to be done up, and in the cockpit the Sutton harness straps slipped on over the top, collected on the No. 1 strap central pin and the fastening clip pushed into its slot in the pin to lock it. From his seat the pilot had all the controls within reach and much of the time flew with his left hand on the throttle and right hand on the spade grip stick with its two machine gun triggers in the centre which could both be pushed by the thumb.

In order that the Gamecock's Jupiter engine should obtain its best performance at height where a fighter needed it, it became necessary to impose a limit on the throttle opening below 5,000 feet (1524 m). This was done on the un-supercharged Jupiter VI by an induction system pressure-operated valve which controlled a linkage in the throttle system. This limited the induction system pressure so that the power output equivalent to 1700 rpm could not be exceeded up to full throttle height. With the fixed pitch propeller the rpm reading was a direct indication of power output. Initial climb at 1700 rpm at sea level would get the Gamecock to 1,500 feet (457 m) in the first minute, and it could climb to 10,000 feet (3048 m) in a little under eight minutes, an average of 1,250 feet (381 m) a minute. This assumes a fairly straight climb to point of interception but a climb to overhead where turning would be necessary would reduce this, so the "book figure" of 20 minutes to 20,000 feet (6096 m) would not often be achieved in practice, especially since the service ceiling of 22,100 feet (6736 m) was the height at which the rate of climb was reduced to 100 feet (30 m) a minute. It should be noted, though, that this performance was comparable to anything else in service at the time.

What was it like to fly the Gamecock? Fifty-six years after its demise no detailed pilot record appears to have been written and whatever recollections any surviving pilots might have would be very dim and distant, but with knowledge of other open cockpit aircraft of the period it is still possible to build up a picture.

The cockpit, typical of fighters of the time, was close-fitting with a simple instrument panel tucked close under the curved coaming. The nearest thing to a "blind flying" instrument was a device rather like a spirit level curved down at the ends and mounted in the centre of the panel below the very prominent central map holder which indicated slip or skid. Most was done on the three basic instruments, airspeed indicator (ASI), altimeter and compass. The altimeter and airspeed indicator had circular dials of about 3.5 in (90 mm) diameter placed close together on the left of the panel where they could both be scanned with a single glance.

Below them were the magneto switches, rather like the then-common household brass capped electric light switch except that there were two switch knobs instead of one. The compass was a bowl type instrument of about six inches (150 mm) diameter mounted centrally below the panel where the pilot could reach forward, release the locking lever, rotate, set and re-lock the grid ring (or "compass card") to set a course or look down on the dial to obtain a reading. On the right side were the previously-mentioned RPM indicator, engine oil pressure gauge and temperature gauge. On the left cockpit wall were the throttle and mixture (or "altitude control") levers together, and on the right side the adjustable tailplane control.

For starting, with chocks in position the stick had to be held right back in the pilot's lap, a standard procedure for tailskid aircraft as on startup the slipstream then pushed on the raised elevator to hold the tail on the ground and resisted the tendency of the propeller thrust to tip the aircraft onto its nose. With the throttle closed and the mixture lever right back in the rich position, fuel cock on the left side of the cockpit turned on and magneto switches off, the propeller was then turned a few revolutions after priming to suck the mixture into the cylinders.

The ground crew member would then call "Contact", and with the throttle open half an inch at the position for tickover the pilot would switch on the magnetos and reply "Contact". The propeller would then be hand swung or turned by Hucks starter until the engine turned over and fired, the pilot checking the oil pressure gauge to ensure rising oil pressure and adjusting the throttle setting to warm the engine at about 800 rpm.

While the engine was warming was a convenient time to make a final check on controls, harness and seat adjustment, this last being important as, regardless of the pilot's height, his eye level had to be right, low enough to be able to read the instruments under the coaming but high enough to retain a good outside view.

Normally all checks would have been done before start-up and pilots on standby would have been able to check their aircraft over thoroughly before signing for its acceptance. During peacetime there was usually plenty of warning for exercises and checks were meticulous and never skimped, so engines could be warmed, ground run and tested with ground crew holding down the tail before flying was due to commence. When ready to taxy, goggles were pulled down, chocks waved away, and with stick held back in the stomach the throttle was eased open to start the aircraft moving forwards, then reduced slightly to avoid undue acceleration while moving on the ground. The aircraft could be steered by the rudder pedals which operated the rudder and the steerable tailskid together, sometimes a short burst of throttle being used to increase the slipstream over the rudder to help in starting a turn.

The take off check was done with the aircraft turned across wind so that any aircraft approaching to land could be seen. Items checked were: throttle friction nut tight (to ensure that if the pilot had to take his hand off the throttle it would not creep back towards the closed position), tailplane trim lever in the neutral position, mixture lever at full rich, magneto switches both on contact, fuel cock on, oil pressure correct and approach and take-off paths clear.

The aircraft was then turned into wind and the throttle opened slowly and smoothly to 1700 rpm for take off. Speed built up rapidly and at little more than 20 mph (32 km/h) the elevator would become effective and the stick could be eased forward slightly to raise the tail and lower the nose so that it was possible to see the take off path ahead. By the time the speed reached 60 mph (97 km/h) the lift of the biplane wings would be such that the Gamecock would be airborne and the pilot would be holding it down to build up 80-90 mph (129-145 km/h) before climbing away.

Exceeding 1700 rpm was not permissible below the full throttle height of 5000 ft (1524 m), and when settled in the climb the tailplane trim lever could be adjusted slightly if necessary to take any out-of-trim loads off the stick. As the aircraft climbed above 5000 ft (1524 m) it was necessary to increase the power setting by opening the throttle further and also weaken the mixture gradually to suit the reduced density of the atmosphere by easing the mixture lever forward just enough to maintain smooth running, thus avoiding fuel wastage from an over-rich mixture.

Levelling off from the climb was by pushing the stick forward until the nose was in the level flight position, that is with the tops of the upper engine cylinders just below the horizon from the pilot's viewpoint, then easing the throttle back to keep the desired cruising or interception revs. The tailplane trim was then moved forward until forward pressure was no longer required on the stick to keep the level attitude. With sufficient hours experience of flying the aircraft this would become automatically accurate without more than an occasional glance at the altimeter.

Like most biplanes with cockpits behind the wings, the view from the cockpit could not be described as particularly good, the view upwards and forwards being obstructed by the top wing and the view downwards and forwards being hidden by the bottom wing. Descending at low speed gave a nose-high attitude in which the view of the ground immediately ahead was largely hidden by the bottom wing, so high speed descents with the nose lowered were probably preferred as they gave a better view ahead. However at speeds above 130 mph (209 km/h) a sharp pull out could result in aileron flutter. Here one must admit to being carried away by this account so - we're going down, pull the mixture lever right back in rich and the throttle lever back about half way, the nose drops with the power no longer holding it up and a little forward speed increases the speed to 120 (193 km/h).

Just a touch of the stick to the left and we're on a curving descent, the patchwork of fields viewed over the left side slowly turning. There's the field, a Gamecock taking off into wind crawls slowly across the grass and is airborne, it shadow moving away from it as it climbs. Now we're down to a couple of thousand feet (600 m) and we put on a bit more power to slow the descent, not looking at the instruments but at the windsock as we track across wind. 800 ft (244 m), open the throttle to cruise position and fly parallel to the windsock pointing downwind.

A curve across wind, speed off to 85 (137 km/h), approach and landing path is clear, reduce power to less than a third, trim lever back to relieve the stick back pressure, straighten out, viewing the grass landing path over the engine, power to a trickle. 200 ft (60 m), stick back a little to reduce speed, 70 mph (113 km/h), over the hedge, stick back a little more, the ground expands around the aircraft, back more, the nose comes up and hides the view in front. Looking well ahead to one side of the nose we're floating just above the grass and can sense the speed dropping off. Keep coming back on the stick, the wheels rumble as they touch the grass, throttle fully closed, the undercarriage takes the weight and the tailskid digs in and slows the aircraft to a walking pace in a hundred yards (91 m).

Rudder across wind and check the approach, hold stick hard back and open throttle enough to start moving against the drag of the tailskid, then reduce it just enough to keep moving at a constant speed back to the hangar. Turn into the wind and close the throttle to come to a stop, switches off. The sudden silence is broken only by the little crackling noises from the engine as it cools down.

Turn off the petrol cock, undo the harness and parachute straps and climb out while the ground crew aircraftman puts the chocks in position under the wheels. Lift out the 'chute and carry it back, sign off on the sheet, the flight is completed.

Summary of Gamecock mods

Gamecock mods were not as extensive as those to the Grebe and were mostly concerned with attempts to cure wing flutter. This saw the addition of an extra pair of vee struts outboard of the interplane struts and the addition of four extra centre-section struts splayed outwards from the front and rear inverted vees, so that late in its service career the Gamecock sported no less than 18 struts (20 including the aileron tie-rods). No wonder it was nicknamed Birdcage and Cock's Cradle. Other changes aimed at preventing flutter were the introduction of new ailerons, longer but with narrower chord, and new rounded wingtips on Gamecock J7910.

On later production Gamecocks in service the upper left side of the cockpit wall was a hinged flap which could be let down to enable the pilot to step in from the side - a great improvement when wearing a parachute. This mod was prompted by comments from pilots and became a standard feature on all the Gloster fighters thereafter. In this they were unique.

Major mods were introduced in further attempts to overcome flutter, such as the introduction of a proper upper wing centre section on the Gamecock II, followed by various changes to fin and rudder and later a significant lengthening of the fuselage.

Gamecock units

3 Squadron
J8034, J8044, J8071, J8074, J8081, J8083, J8407, J8408, J8410, J8411, J8412, J8417.

17 Squadron
Only recorded serials are J8405, J8408, J8414.

23 Squadron
J7892, J7893, J7894, J7895, J7896, J7897, J7898, J7899, J7901, J7902, J7903, J7904, J7905, J7907, J7910, J7912, J7913, J7914, J7915, J7916, J8034, J8036, J8039, J8040, J8041, J8044, J8045, J8046, J8071, J8073, J8074, J8075, J8076, J8077, J8078, J8080, J8082, J8083, J8084, J8085, J8089, J8091, J8092, J8093, J8094, J8095, J8406, J8408, J8409, J8410, J8412, J8415, J8420, J8421.

32 Squadron
J7907, J7909, J8042, J8043, J8044, J8069, J8070, J8072, J8073, J8074, J8080, J8081, J8087, J8091, J8420.

43 Squadron
J7900, J7904, J7905, J7906, J7907, J7908, J7909, J7911, J7914, J7918, J7919, J7920, J8034, J8035, J8036, J8037, J8038, J8090, J8095, J8414, J8415, J8416, J8417, J8418, J8420, J8421.

19 Squadron
J8035 only.

Flying Training Schools
2 FTS J8076. 3 FTS J8089.

Armament & Gunnery School
J8033, J8072, J8073, J8088.

Central Flying School
J7900 (DC), J8046, J8047, J8074, J8076, J8089, J8093.

RAF Cranwell
J8077

Home Aircraft Depot Station Flight
J7920.

Home Communications Flight
J8036, J8073, J8085, J8088, J8413.

Andover Communications Flight
J8088.

Gamecock contracts

The Gamecock first feature in the Gloucestershire Aircraft Company's accounts as production machines in their financial year 1925-26, which ended on 5 May. There is no mention of the three prototypes or civil Gamecock G-EBNT.

Year ended:					
5 May 1926	30 machines	£79,555	Production	£2,652 each
	Spares	£13,340	Spares	
5 May 1927	62 machines	£145,665	Production	£2,349 each
	1 machine	£850	Reconditioning	
	Spares	£16,332	Spares	
5 May 1928	2 machines	£3,931	Production?	£1,965 each
	Spares	£11,818	Spares	
	Modifications	£5,968	Modifications	
5 May 1929	10 machines	£16,450	Reconditioning	
	Spares	£6,908	Spares	
	Modifications	£11,870	Modifications	
5 May 1930	Spares	£4,594	Spares	
	Modifications	£2,310	Modifications	
5 May 1931	Spares	£4,486	Spares	
	Modifications	£195	Modifications	
5 May 1932	Spares	£376	Spares	
Sub-totals		£229,151	Production (94)	
		£57,854	Spares	
		£17,300	Reconditioning	
		£20,343	Modifications	
TOTAL		£324,648		

The 94 machines listed here are accounted for by the two RAF orders, for 30 and 60 machines, plus Gamecock II J8804, the two pattern aircraft for Finland and the one-off J9248.

Gamecock production summary

Total production 98

Three Prototypes:

J7497 Gloucestershire Gamecock ordered on Contract No 504577/24 (398 hp Jupiter IV) (297 kW).
J7756 and J7757 Two Gloucestershire Gamecocks ordered on Contract No 571417/25 (398 hp Jupiter IV) (297 kW).

90 production aircraft for RAF:

J7891 to J 7920 30 Gloucestershire Gamecocks Mk I ordered on Contract No 606962/25 dated September 1925 to Specification 18/25. 425 hp (317 kW) Jupiter VI.

J8033 to J8047 First 15 of 60 Gloster Gamecocks Mk I ordered in three parts on Contract No 664493/26 dated July 1926. 425 hp (317 kW) Jupiter VI.

J8069 to J8095 Next 27 of 60 Gloster Gamecocks Mk I ordered on Contract No 664493/26 (Part 2) dated July 1926. 425 hp (317 kW) Jupiter VI.

J8405 to J8422 Final 18 of 60 Gloster Gamecocks Mk I ordered on Contract No 664493/26 (Part 3) dated November 1926. 425 hp (317 kW) Jupiter VI.

Other British military Gamecocks:

J7959 All metal Gamecock project to be built by Boulton & Paul ordered on Contract No 633677/25. Cancelled.

J8804 Gloster Gamecock Mk II ordered on Contract No 735063/26 dated January 1928. 425 hp (317 kW) Jupiter VI.

J9248 Gloster Gamecock Mk II ordered on Contract No 827757/28. 495 hp (369 kW) Orion. Originally civil-registered as G-EBOE on 20 May 1926 to Gloster. To RAE 10 June 1929, crashed at Bagshot 9 August 1929.

Two Gloster-built pattern aircraft for Finland:
GA-38 original short fuselage version, similar to J8804.
GA-43 long-fuselage version, similar to Gamecock "III" J8047.

15 *Kukko* production aircraft built in Finland:
GA-44 to 47 4 *Kukkos* built by Finnish National Aircraft Factory as first Finnish production batch.
GA-48 to 58 11 *Kukkos* built by Finnish National Aircraft Factory as second Finnish production batch.

Civil Gamecocks:

G-EBNT Gloster civil demonstrator registered 17 March 1926. Transferred to RAF as J8033 March 1927.
G-EBOE registered 20 May 1926. Not taken up, cancelled 19 March 1928. Later completed for RAF with serial J9248 (see above).
G-ADIN registered 3 June 1935. Formerly J8047.

Gamecock details

Single seat fighter to Specification 37/23 (three prototypes) and 18/25 (90 production Gamecock I). Also one civil, two Mk II and two pattern aircraft for Finland.

Construction: wooden wings and fuselage, fabric covered, with metal forward fuselage panels.

Engine:
First and second prototypes: 398 hp (297 kW) Bristol Jupiter IV with 8 ft 8 in (2.64 m) dia. Watts propeller.
Gamecock I and II: 425 hp (317 kW) Bristol Jupiter VI with 9 ft (2.74 m) dia. Watts propeller.
J8075: 450 hp (336 kW) Bristol Mercury IIA with 8 ft 10 in (2.69 m) dia. Hele-Shaw Beacham VP propeller.
J 8047: 450 hp (336 kW) Bristol Jupiter VII with Hele-Shaw Beacham VP propeller.
J8047 (and as G-ADIN): 490 hp (366 kW) Bristol Jupiter VIIIFP.

Armament: two .303 (7.7 mm) Vickers Mk I machine guns on either side of fuselage. Provision for four 20 lb (9 kg) bombs under fuselage.

Dimensions:

Gamecock I: Span upper wing 29 ft 9.5 in (9.08 m), lower wing 25 ft 11 in (7.9 m). Length 19 ft 8 in (5.99 m). Height 9 ft 8 in (2.95 m). Wing area 264 sq ft (24.5 sq m).

Gamecock II: Span upper wing 30 ft 1 in (9.17 m), lower wing 26 ft 4.5 in (8.04 m). Length 19 ft 10.5 in (6.06 m). Height 9 ft 11 in (3.02 m). Wing area 268 sq ft (24.9 sq m).

Performance and weights:

Gamecock I: Top speed 154 mph (248 km/h) at sea level, 145 mph (233 km/h) at 10,000 ft (3048 m). Climb to 20,000 ft (6096 m) 27 min. Service ceiling 22,100 ft (6736 m). Weight loaded 2742 lb (1244 kg), tare 1930 lb (875 kg).

Gamecock II: Top speed 157 mph (253 km/h) at 5,000 ft (1524 m). Climb to 15,000 ft (4572 m) 13.3 min. Service ceiling 21,600 ft (6584 m). Weight loaded 3082 lb (1398 kg), tare 2050 lb (930 kg).

Gamecock J9248 with 495 hp (369 kW) Bristol Orion: climb to 20,000 ft (6096 m) less than 13 min.

Kukko ("Cock") (Finnish Gamecock II)

Single-seat interceptor. Two pattern aircraft built by Gloster Aircraft Company: GA-38 (short fuselage), GA-43 (long fuselage). 15 long fuselage version built by Finnish National Aircraft Factory, Helsinki: GA-44 to 58. Interchangeable wheel or ski undercarriage.

Construction: wooden fuselage and wings, fabric covered, with metal forward fuselage panels.

Engine: Gnome-Rhone licence-built Jupiter IV. Initially IVA 9Ab and 9Ak of 420 hp (313 kW), later IV 9Ag of 480 hp (358 kW).

Armament: two .303 in (7.7 mm) machine guns in troughs on the fuselage sides. Provision for four 9 kg bombs.

Dimensions: Span upper wing 30 ft 1 in (9.17 m), lower wing 26 ft 6 in (8.08 m). Length (initial short fuselage version GA-38) 19 ft 10.5 in (6.06 m). Length (production version) 22 ft 0.5 in (6.7 m). Height 10 ft 2 in (3.1 m). Wing area 295 sq ft (27.4 sq m).

Performance and weights: (Martlesham figures for Gamecock II J8804)

Top speed 157 mph (253 km/h) at 5,000 ft (1524 m). Climb to 15,000 ft (4572 m) 13.3 min. Service ceiling 21,600 ft (6584 m). All up weight loaded 3082 lb (1398 kg), tare 2050 lb (930 kg).

Gamecock structure details

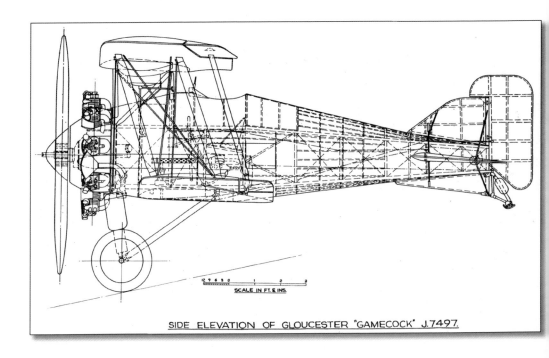

SCALE IN FT. & INS.

SIDE ELEVATION OF GLOUCESTER "GAMECOCK" J.7497.

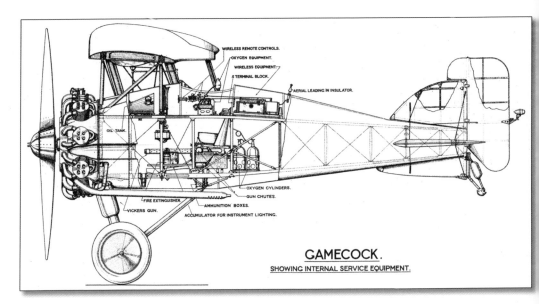

WIRELESS REMOTE CONTROLS.
OXYGEN EQUIPMENT.
WIRELESS EQUIPMENT.
6 TERMINAL BLOCK.
AERIAL LEADING IN INSULATOR.
OIL TANK.
OXYGEN CYLINDERS.
GUN CHUTES.
FIRE EXTINGUISHER.
AMMUNITION BOXES.
VICKERS GUN.
ACCUMULATOR FOR INSTRUMENT LIGHTING.

GAMECOCK.
SHOWING INTERNAL SERVICE EQUIPMENT.

Engine bearer bulkhead.

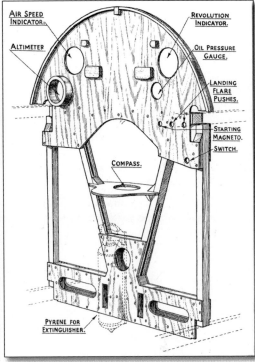

Instrument board bulkhead.

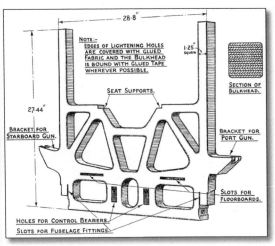

Bulkhead No. 4.

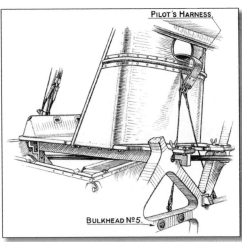

Seat.

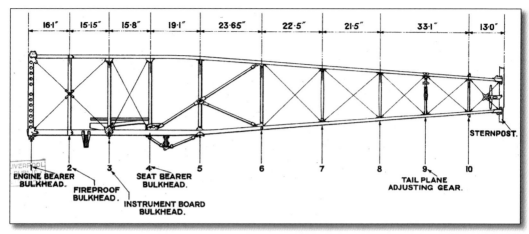

Fuselage showing strut numbering.

Oleo leg.

Axle end with fitting and fairing.

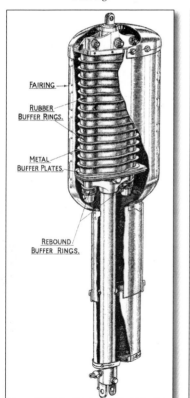

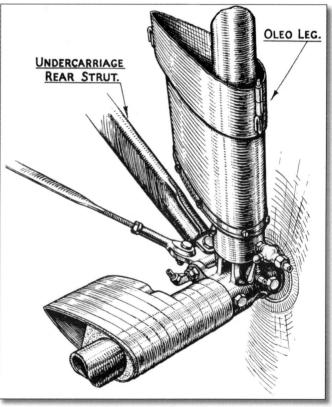

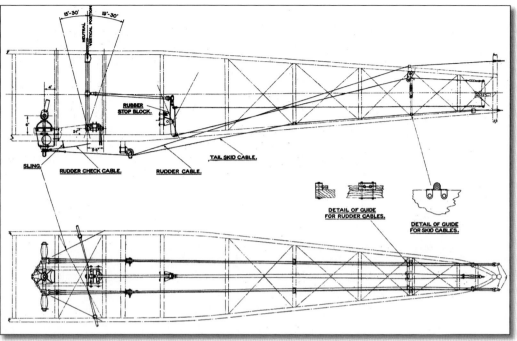

General arrangement of flying controls.

Tail skid.

Tail plane control lever in cockpit.

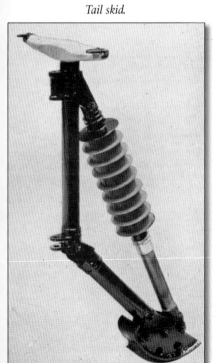

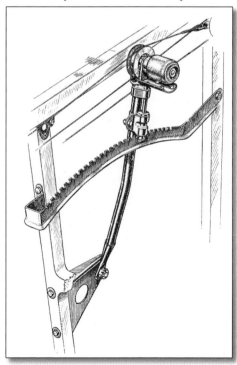

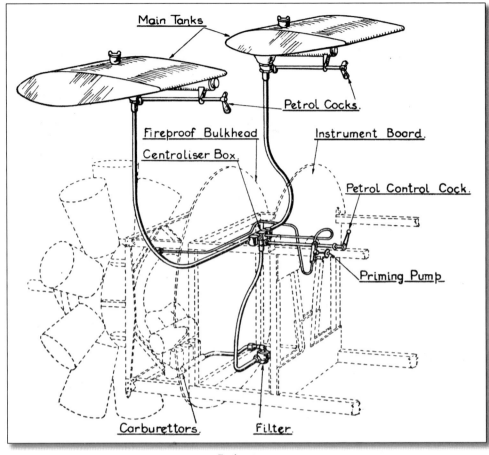

Main Tanks

Petrol Cocks.

Fireproof Bulkhead

Instrument Board.

Centraliser Box

Petrol Control Cock.

Priming Pump

Carburettors.

Filter.

Fuel system.

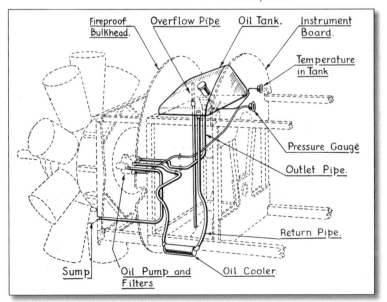

Fireproof Bulkhead.

Overflow Pipe

Oil Tank.

Instrument Board.

Temperature in Tank

Pressure Gauge

Outlet Pipe.

Return Pipe.

Sump

Oil Pump and Filters

Oil Cooler.

Oil system.

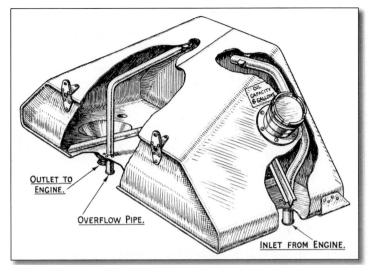

Oil tank.

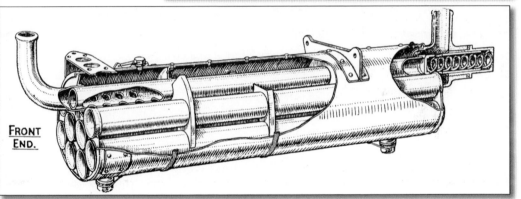

Oil cooler.

Ammunition boxes.

Seat.

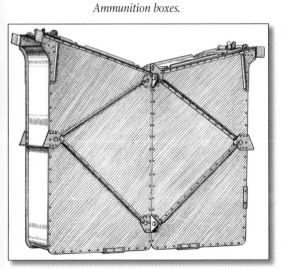

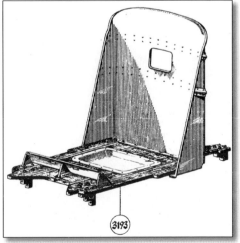

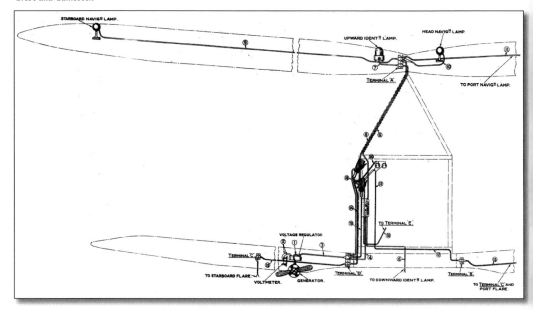

Wiring diagram for electrical services A.

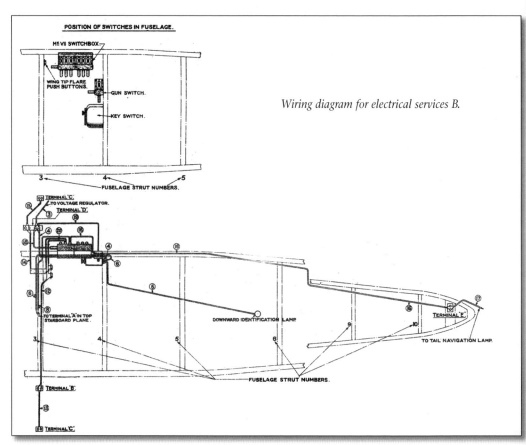

Wiring diagram for electrical services B.

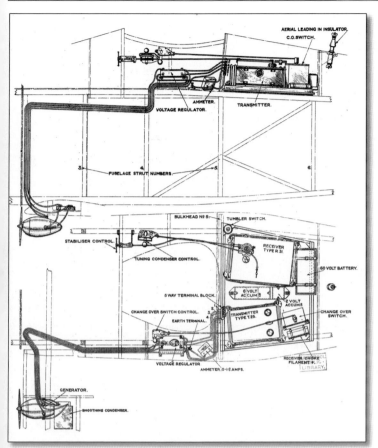

Layout of wireless equipment.

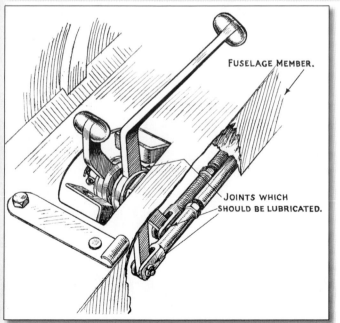

Engine control levers on top longeron in cockpit.

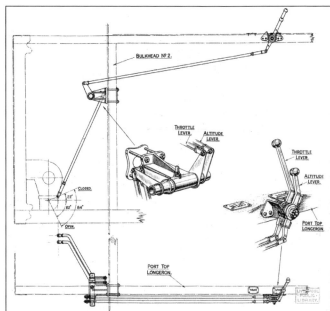

Engine controls.

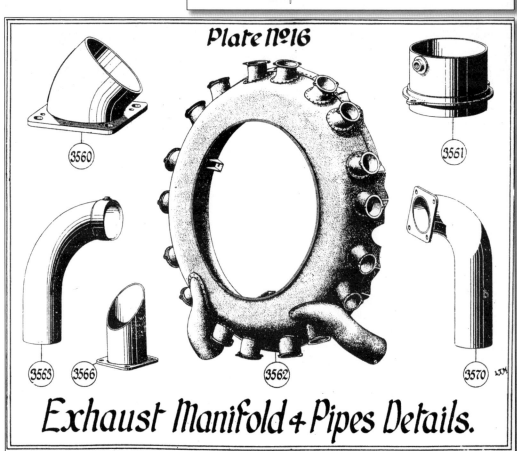

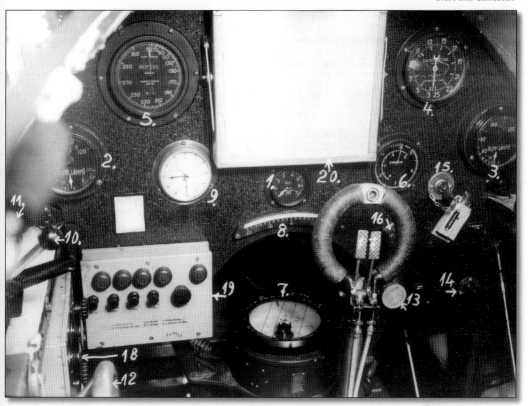

The only known photograph of a Gamecock instrument panel depicts the Finnish version with metal panel and modified switch box. Otherwise it is very similar to the RAF version.

1. Oil pressure gauge (S Smith & Sons)
2. Oil temperature gauge, returning
3. Oil temperature gauge, outgoing
4. Tachometer (Delta)
5. Airspeed indicator (S Smith & Sons)
6. Altimeter
7. Compass
8. Bank indicator
9. Clock
10. Throttle lever

11. Auxiliary air lever
12. Stabiliser control
13. Primer (Kigas)
14. Oil and fuel cock
15. Booster magneto switch (in contact position)
16. Booster magneto crank
17. Machine gun triggers
18. Main fuse box
19. Main switch box
20. Map case

Heated suit (just below 15).
Labels "Open" to left of and "Closed" above 14.
Ignition switch and extinguisher not shown on photo.

Grateful thanks to Sten-Olof Niemenen of Suomen Ilmailumuseo (The Finnish Aviation Museum) for photograph and key. (Via Jet Age Museum)

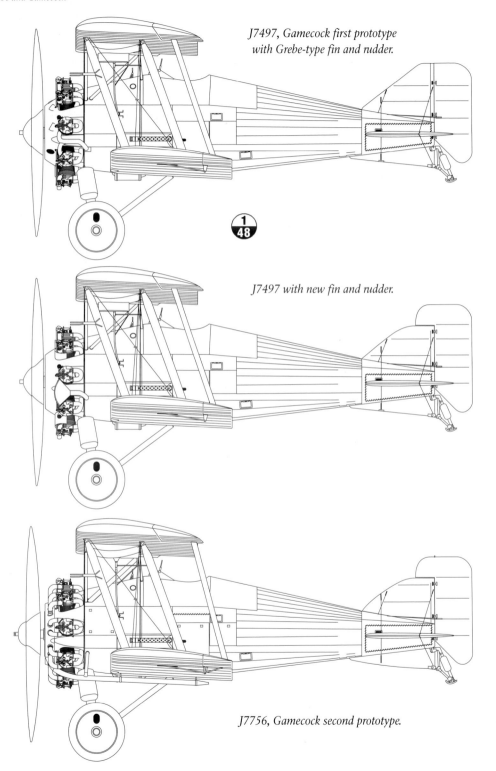

*J7497, Gamecock first prototype
with Grebe-type fin and rudder.*

J7497 with new fin and rudder.

J7756, Gamecock second prototype.

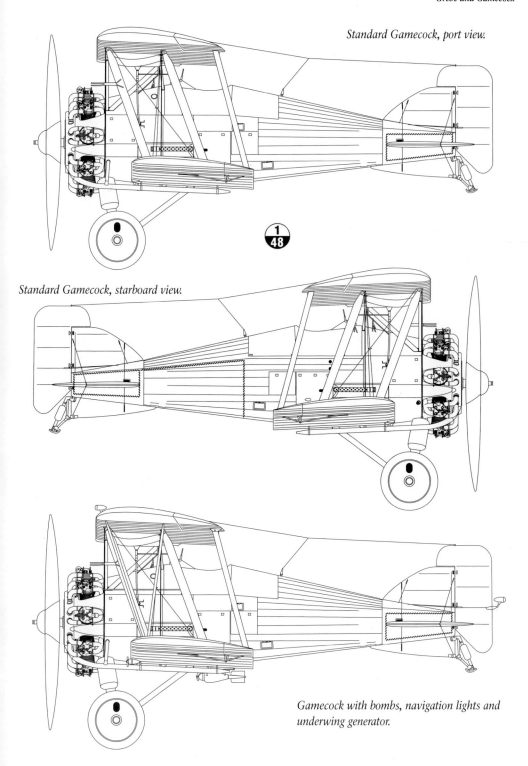

Standard Gamecock, port view.

Standard Gamecock, starboard view.

Gamecock with bombs, navigation lights and underwing generator.

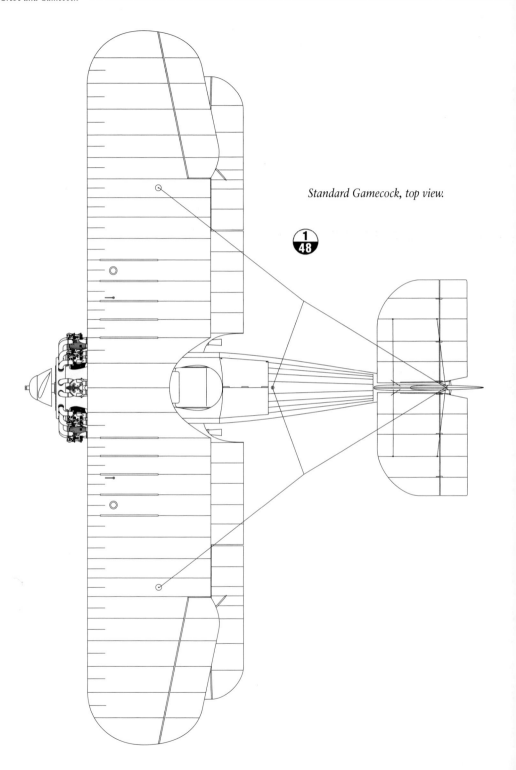

Standard Gamecock, top view.

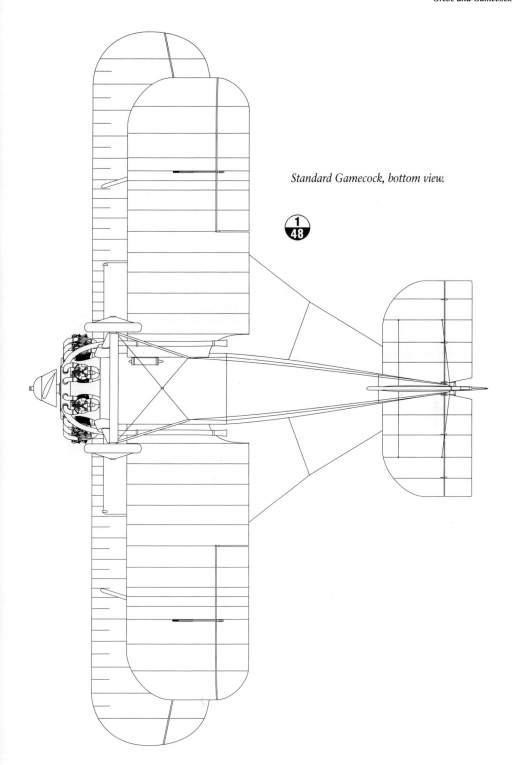

Standard Gamecock, bottom view.

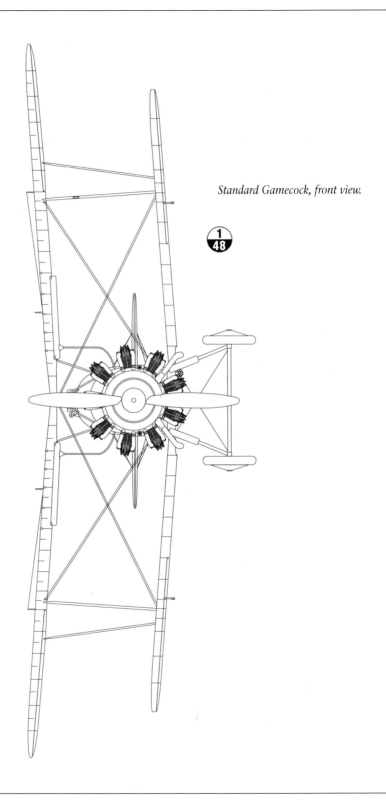

Standard Gamecock, front view.

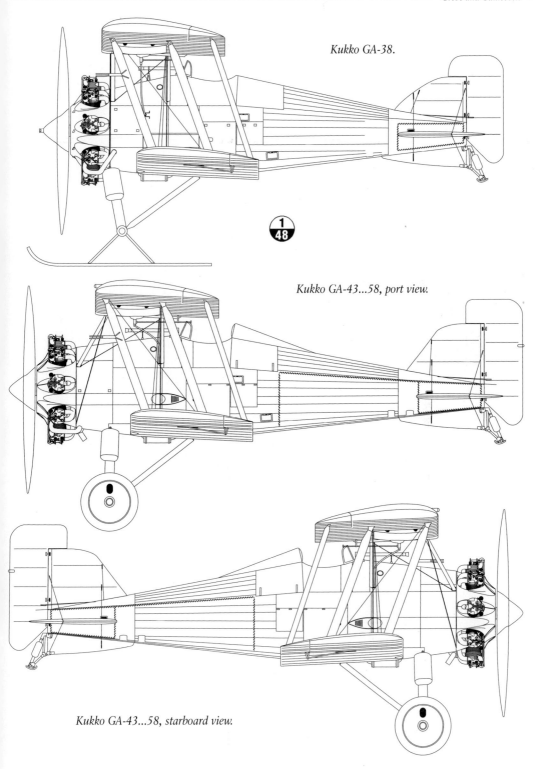

Kukko GA-38.

Kukko GA-43...58, port view.

Kukko GA-43...58, starboard view.

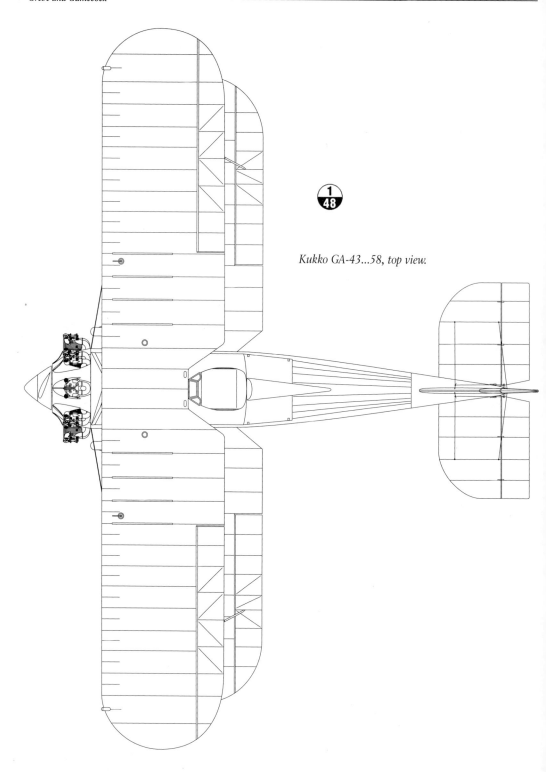

Kukko GA-43...58, top view.

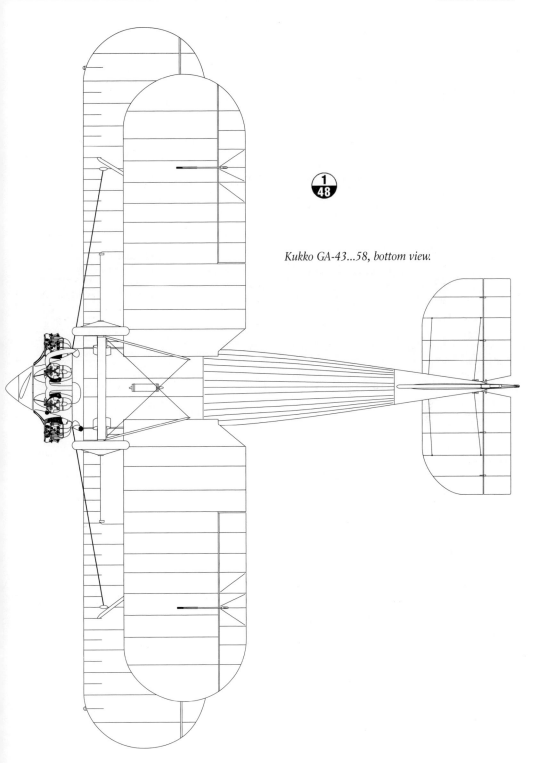

Kukko GA-43...58, bottom view.

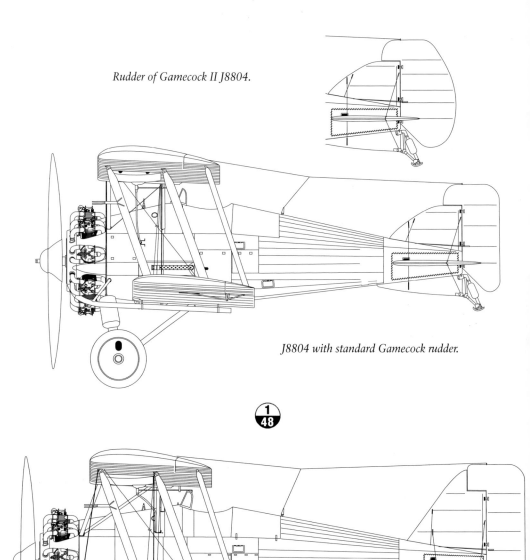

Rudder of Gamecock II J8804.

J8804 with standard Gamecock rudder.

Gamecock "III" J8047.

Grebe and Gamecock developments

Gorcock

Folland had put the Gloster Company firmly on the map with his Mars I racer, better known as the Bamel. This was basically a hotrod Nighthawk with powerful Napier Lion 12-cylinder engine. It won the Aerial Derby in 1921, 1922 and (as the Gloster I) in 1923. Following these successes, the Air Ministry became interested in a Lion-engined version of the Grebe.

This became the Gloucestershire Gorcock and it was developed more or less in parallel with the Gamecock, not as a development of it. The Gorcock was built to Specification 24/23 and the Gamecock to Specification 37/23. The serials of the three Gorcocks, J7501-3, were earlier in sequence than all Gamecocks except the first prototype.

The first Gorcock, J7501, was delivered in 1927 powered by the 450 hp (336 kW) geared Lion IV, giving it a higher thrust line than the ungeared version. It was the only one of the three to have the reverse-tapered ailerons with forward-sloping hinge line of the early Grebe. Due to the engine bulkhead for the Lion being set back under the top wing like the Bamel to avoid nose-heaviness, the base of the front inverted vee struts supporting the upper wings on their centre line had to be attached further back as well, making them lean forward at the top like the Gloster I. Another noticeable difference from the Grebe was that the tailplane was not mounted mid-fuselage but on top of it, a feature which was developed further in the Goldfinch.

The first Gorcock, J7501, in its early configuration with wooden propeller, circular-section radiator, tapered ailerons, SE5-type fin and rudder and high-set tailplane. (Author's collection)

Another shot of Gorcock J7501 in its early configuration. (Author's collection)

J7501 at Martlesham, still with wooden propeller but now unarmed and with angled, parallel-chord ailerons. The gun breech fairing has also been modified. (Author's collection)

The second Gorcock, J7502, at Brockworth, still with SE5-type fin and rudder but with metal propeller. (Author's collection)

J7502 at Martlesham, with wireless aerial fitted. (Author's collection, above and via Phil Butler, below)

J7502 at Martlesham, with wireless aerial fitted. (Via Phil Butler)

J7502 back at Brockworth, now with enlarged fin and rudder and with radiator cross-section semi-circular. (Via Jack Meaden)

J7502 back at Brockworth, now with enlarged fin and rudder and with radiator cross-section semi-circular. (Author's collection, above and via JD Oughton, below)

Howard Saint shows off Gorcock J7502 for Flight's photographer. (Flight, from author's collection)

Between the undercarriage legs was the Lion's cylindrical radiator, coned to a point at the front with moveable tapered radial shutters to control the amount of cooling air being used. This echoed the Lamblin radiator of the Bamel and Gloster I.

Another experimental feature being developed was metal construction. J7501 had a metal fuselage and wooden wings, all fabric covered except for light alloy cowlings. The propeller was wooden and the engine cowling and carburettor intakes were of similar form to the Gloster I, but the right hand side exhaust manifold from the top bank of cylinders now had two outlets, one to each pair of cylinders instead of one for the whole bank, intended to increase service life.

Machine guns were in the fuselage sides as in the Gamecock, with troughs running forward along the cowlings. A metal blister was tried out at the side of the cockpit at one stage to give the pilot better access to the machine gun breeches. After trials at Martlesham in August and September 1925, modifications by Gloster followed and it eventually went to the RAE at Farnborough on 16 May 1928. On 4 September 1929 it broke up in the air over Aldershot. The pilot baled out safely.

J7502 followed quickly, also having a metal fuselage and wooden wings and initially having the same type tail unit and radiator as J7501. The ailerons were attached to the same sloping hinge line but were now parallel-sided and of increased area as on the later production Grebes and the Gamecock I, providing the familiar "kink" in the trailing edge. The engine was a Lion VIII of 525 hp (392 kW) which was ungeared, giving a lower thrust line. The three rows of cylinders had shorter exhaust stubs which were now closely faired-in. A metal propeller with pointed spinner was fitted, similar to that on the Gloster III racing seaplane.

Gloster hoped to enter a Gorcock in the 1926 King's Cup Air Race but this was not permitted. The new fighter did appear at the 1926 RAF Display, however, as one of four new fighter types. It was flown by Flg Off Sorley, *"although he had had very little time on the machine to be fully conversant with its feel. He succeeded, however, in showing to great effect the remarkable manoeuvrability and climbing qualities of the latest Gloster Scout"*. This was J7502, the Gorcock with direct drive Napier VIII engine, bearing the New Types number 4. The company stated proudly in its house magazine The Gloster: *"This machine differs from its competitors in that it fulfils all the Air Ministry's requirements and secures its brilliant performance with full equipment. Thus wing radiators with their comparative vulnerability and unreliability have been avoided. The radiator is of a semicircular form and fixed to the body of the machine between forward struts of the undercarriage and can be easily detached. All equipment and controls are easily accessible for inspection and easily removed."*

With continuing development a number of changes took place on J7502 and in its next form it had a tall balanced rudder like Gamecock "III" J8047. The leading edge of the fin was not, like J8047, moved forward to increase its area, the sloping front of the Grebe-type fin merely being continued upwards to meet the rudder balance.

The radiator now had the upper half removed and the lower half moved up against the bottom of the engine cowl, so that viewed from head-on it was a semicircular bulge below the engine with a 50 per cent reduction in frontal area, indicating that detailed examination of cooling requirements was resulting in system improvements.

The Gorcock's clean lines now made it a good looking fighter and advantage was taken of this when in February 1927 Howard Saint flew it in a demonstration for press photographers. Flight's editor was obviously impressed and accompanied a spread of photographs with an article which recognised the benefits obtained by Gloster's experience with racing aircraft. From March to November it was at Martlesham, then went to the RAE at Farnborough for propeller tests in 1928, ending its days there with a crash landing on 27 May 1931.

By contrast, the third Gorcock J7503, which was to be all metal, obtained little publicity and was overtaken by the Goldfinch. There seems to be no photographic evidence of J7503 in completed form. The only photograph published which claimed to be the all-metal J7503 with parallel chord ailerons, in Derek James's *Gloster Aircraft Since 1917*, has been clearly identified as J7501 with the early reverse-tapered ailerons, original engine cowlings and wooden propeller, so whether the metal wings of J7503 were similar to the later "metal Gamecock" or Goldfinch with a centre section in the top wing is uncertain. Although reported to have been completed and used for trials, little positive information seems to have been released by the company on J7503

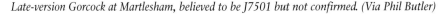

Late-version Gorcock at Martlesham, believed to be J7501 but not confirmed. (Via Phil Butler)

or its metal wing. It went to Martlesham in April 1927, where it suffered a piston failure, returned briefly to Gloster and was back at Martlesham between June and September and again in 1928.

The Gorcock was 20 mph (32 km/h) faster than the Gamecock I but it was experimental only, still suffered from wing flutter and was overtaken by later developments. The main purpose was in developing a high-speed fighter with the Lion engine. It was a difficult engine, though. Gloster's chief inspector Basil Fielding wrote: "*We had a lot of trouble in getting even running on all three engine blocks and spent hours cutting the air intakes at different angles. This also necessitated carrying out a lot of running after dark when flame colour could be seen. The trouble was eventually cured.*" While no production fighter would use the Lion, the information provided was useful in the design of the later Lion-engined Gloster racing seaplanes.

Gorcock details

Single-seat interceptor. Three prototypes only, J7501, J7502 and J7503, ordered on Contract No 452554/24 of May 1924 to Specification 24/23 (later 7/24).

Construction: J7501 and J7502: steel fuselage and wooden wings, fabric covered. J7503: all steel, fabric covered.

Engine:
J75012 and J7503: geared Napier Lion IV of 450 hp (336 kW) with 9 ft (2.74 m) dia. wooden propeller.
J7502: direct-drive Napier Lion VIII of 525 hp (392 kW) with 9 ft 2 in (2.79 m) wooden or metal propeller.

Armament: two .303 (7.7 mm) Vickers machine guns in troughs on the fuselage sides. Provision for four 20 lb (9 kg) Cooper bombs on light series carrier Mk 1.

Dimensions: Span, upper wing 28 ft 6 in (8.69 m), lower wing 25 ft 0 in (7.62 m). Length 26 ft 1 in (7.95 m). Height 10 ft 3 in (3.12 m). Wing area 250 sq ft (23.2 sq m).

Performance and weights:
J7501 and J7502: top speed 164 mph (264 km/h) at 5,000 ft (1524 m). Climb to 15,000 ft (4572 m) 11 min. Service ceiling 24,000 ft (7315 m). Weight loaded 3,179 lb (1442 kg), tare 2,346 lb (1064 kg).
J7503: top speed 174 mph (280 km/h) at 5,000 ft (1524 m). Climb to 15,000 ft (4572 m) 10.5 min. Service ceiling 24,000 ft (7315 m). Weight loaded 3,337 lb (1514 kg), tare 2,422 lb (1099 kg).

Goldfinch

Gloster's Goldfinch was a metal version of the Gamecock, the RAF's last wooden fighter. In its developed form it was intended as a successor to the RAF's Gamecocks and Siskins but it lost out to the Bristol Bulldog, as described below. Only one was built.

A one-off Air Ministry order was placed with Boulton & Paul for a metal Gamecock project under contract no. 633677/25. The serial J7959 was allocated but the project was cancelled - at what stage is not known. Boulton & Paul was one of the most advanced builders of all-metal aircraft at the time, but it seems that with Gloster's acquisition of the Steel Wing Co the project was brought back in house.

Gloster's "all-metal Gamecock", as the Air Ministry initially referred to it, was ordered to Specification 16/25 and given the name Goldfinch. The fuselage structure was, in fact, partially wooden. Photographs of an uncovered mostly-metal framework without propeller were not published until 1928, but the Goldfinch had already flown in May 1927 and gone to Martlesham the same month. This uncovered framework in the photos has usually been regarded as a Gloster-built structure, but Philip Jarrett (Aeroplane Monthly, January 1997) speculates that it may have been the airframe of Boulton & Paul's cancelled J7959.

Apart from the metal structure this first version had a Gamecock II-style top wing with a Gamecock I-style fuselage, engine, undercarriage and tail, but with one notable alteration: the tailplane and elevator assembly had been moved up to the top of the fuselage. The reason for this change is not known but Jack Meaden writes that it was probably made to try to reduce the effects of the fuselage shielding the control surfaces from the airflow during spin recovery.

With serial J7940 the Goldfinch came back to Gloster in July 1927 and was modified to have a supercharged engine, the 450 hp (336 kW) Jupiter VIIF fitted with stub exhausts, pointed spinner and faired nose. The fin was also extended forward along the top of the fuselage to about twice its original length, the raised tailplane was given semicircular tips matching the top wing, and the span of the bottom wing was increased by inserting

The skeleton of the first Goldfinch, referred to in 1928 as the "Gamecock II, All Metal". Its exhaust collector ring differs from the standard Gamecock. (Via Jack Meaden)

The view from the rear shows the high-mounted tailplane identifying it as the Goldfinch, not the Gamecock II.
(Author's collection)

an extended wing root which was faired into the fuselage and not cut away as in the Gamecock. This had the effect of moving the bottom attachment of the interplane struts outboard in line with the tops so that they no longer leaned outward but had now become upright.

The lower wingtips remained square with rounded corners like the Gamecock I, not being made semicircular as in the Gamecock II. The effect of the increase in span of the lower wing was to make it only 2 ft 2 in (660 mm) less than the 30 ft (9.144 m) span of the upper wing.

Jack Meaden examined some of the changes that had taken place during the five years 1923-28 in the Grebe-Gamecock-Goldfinch line. Span of the top wing had increased very little, from 29 ft 4 in through 29 ft 9 in to 30 ft 0 in (8.941 / 9.068 / 9.144 m) but the bottom wing span had increased by nearly three feet (915 mm), from 25 ft 0 in through 25 ft 11 in to 27 ft 10 in (7.62 / 7.9 / 8.484 m).

The result was a steady increase in wing area in two 10 sq ft (0.929 sq m) jumps, from 254 through 264 to 274 sq ft (23.6 / 24.53 / 25.45 sq m). The need for this was apparent from the increases in loaded weight, from 2538 through 2742 to 3236 lb (1151.2 / 1243.8 / 1467.8 kg), a total increase of almost 700 lb (317 kg). This was accompanied by a power increase of 50 hp (37 kW) and supercharging, increasing the operational ceiling by 4,000 ft (1220 m) to 27,000 ft (8230 m) and the maximum speed by 20 mph (32 km/h) to 171.5 mph (276 km/h) at 10,000 ft (3048 m).

The final changes to Goldfinch J7940 incorporated the features developed on Gamecock "III" J8047: the lengthened fuselage, the upright undercarriage with increased track, the taller fin and rudder of increased area and (the only other machine to have this feature) the added tip to the fin which gave an unbroken line to the vertical tail surfaces. Differences from the Gamecock included reduced dihedral on the lower wing only, resulting in longer interplane struts and greater gap at the wingtips. Also the fuselage attachment points of the two front centre section struts were moved back from the top of the engine bulkhead to the fireproof bulkhead, making the struts upright instead of sloping.

The metal structure had high tensile steel wing spars, two types being tried. The first "metal Gamecock" airframe had "triple-tube" spars consisting of three tubes one above the other with continuous webs rolled from strip. The second type was the Gloster "lattice girder" spar and this was used on the Goldfinch in its later form in the upper wing only.

The modified Goldfinch photographed at Brockworth, now with enlarged fin, guns fitted and re-engined without collector ring. (Author's collection)

This view shows the extended lower wing root of the Goldfinch. (Jet Age Museum/Russell Adams Collection)

Goldfinch J7940 at Martlesham. (Via JD Oughton, above and author's collection, below)

Modified again, J7940 with the tall fin and rudder as fitted to Gamecock "III" J8047. (Author's collection)

The ribs had a Warren girder type of bracing and the fuselage was of plate-jointed steel tubes with the body shape rounded off by spruce formers and stringers. The whole was fabric covered except for the light alloy nose fairings and covering behind the engine, and the overall result was a good looking aeroplane that Howard Saint made the most of when he showed it off in one of his low-level displays late in 1928. The object was to advertise it, no doubt in the hope of interesting possible overseas purchasers, the Bristol Bulldog having won the F9/26 competition in spite of generally good results for the Goldfinch at the 1927 Martlesham trials. Although rated as "markedly superior" to the Gamecock in performance, it was criticised as uncomfortable, heavy on the controls, draughty and having a poor view.

The Bulldog was a new design with development capability ahead of it. In fact it was not supplied to F9/26 but became the Bulldog II with Jupiter VII engine supplied to a new specification, F17/28, and later the Bulldog IIA with Jupiter VIIF supplied to F11/29.

The design of the Goldfinch, based on the Gamecock II, had its major features settled before F9/26 was issued, so all the "stretch" in the basic design had been taken up. All the same its general performance was not significantly different from the Bulldog and load was similar, four 20 lb (9 kg) bombs being the same and the two machine guns having 500 rounds each, only 100 less than the Bulldog. Where it lost out was on endurance, the Bulldog having adopted a similar type of wing fuel tanks but with 70 gallons (318 l) instead of 57 (259 l).

The Jupiter VIIF had a fuel consumption of which varied from 16 gallons (73 l) per hour at cruise to 37 gallons (168 l) per hour at maximum performance setting. Allowing for one hour at maximum power for climb and combat, the Goldfinch had an endurance of two hours against the Bulldog's three.

The Goldfinch's career ended when it crashed on landing at Farnborough in October 1929 so J7940 remained the only Goldfinch. In producing it much was learned about metal construction and production which was of great value for later Gloster aircraft.

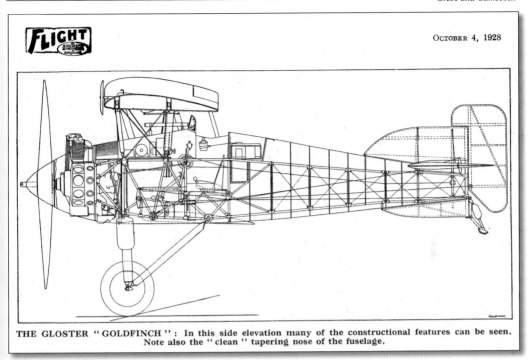

THE GLOSTER " GOLDFINCH " : In this side elevation many of the constructional features can be seen. Note also the " clean " tapering nose of the fuselage.

Flight ran a major feature on the Goldfinch in October 1928 which included this drawing of the internal arrangement. (Flight, from author's collection)

Goldfinch details

Single-seat high-altitude interceptor, essentially a metal Gamecock II. One prototype only, J7940, ordered on Contract No 633678/25 dated January 1926 to Specification 16/25. Later modified to Specification 9/26.

Construction: Initially wood and metal fuselage with metal wings and tail, fabric covered. Later, all metal except for spruce fuselage formers and stringers, fabric covered.

Engine: Initially Bristol Jupiter V of 436 hp (325 kW).
Later Bristol Jupiter VIIF (supercharged) of 450 hp (336 kW) with 9 ft (2.74 m) dia. Watts wooden propeller.

Armament: two .303 (7.7 mm) Vickers Mk 1 machine guns in troughs on the fuselage sides.

Dimensions: Span 30 ft (9.14 m). Length 22 ft 3 in (6.78 m). Height 10 ft 6 in (3.2 m). Wing area 274.3 sq ft (25.5 sq m).

Performance and weights: Top speed 172 mph (277 km/h) at 10,000 ft (3048 m), 157.5 mph (253 km/h) at 15,000 ft (4572 m). Climb to 10,000 ft (3048 m) 7 min 20 sec, to 20,000 ft (6096 m) 16 min. Service ceiling 26,900 ft (8199 m). Weight loaded 3,236 lb (1468 kg), tare 2,058 lb (934 kg).

Guan

Further experimental programmes continued in 1926 with the Guan, two of which were built with serials J7722 and J7723 for the purpose of testing the use of exhaust driven turbo-superchargers in high altitude operations.

Both Guan airframes were similar to Gorcock J7502 in its later form, again with the high-mounted tailplane and the semicircular radiator under the fuselage, except that the rudder height was not increased and the wing span was greater by 3 ft 4 in (1016 mm), becoming 31 ft 10 in (9.7 m). It was not intended to be thrown about like an operational fighter and the top wing overhang was not braced. Both had impressive external plumbing: J7722 had a 450 hp (336 kW) geared Napier Lion IV engine with the turbocharger mounted below the propeller shaft, and J7723 had a 525 hp (392 kW) direct drive Lion V with the turbocharger mounted on top of the engine. In both cases the exhaust pipe on each side was led forward to the turbocharger with its complicated piping system.

J7722 first flew in August 1926 and went to Farnborough on 20 September. J7723 was not completed until early the following year and went to Farnborough for testing on 8 April 1927. The turbocharger system was still being developed and its troubles resulted in continual hold-ups, putting the programme back, but not before a maximum speed of 155 mph (249 km/h) was achieved at 16,000 ft (4877 m), with a service ceiling of 31,000 ft (9449 m).

Advantage was taken of the high altitude performance to carry out further tests of the Hele-Shaw Beacham constant-speed variable-pitch propeller on J7723. Further development of the Guan included a third machine, J7724, which was to have had a Napier Lioness engine, but the programme was cancelled and it was not completed. J7722 last flew on 6 December 1927 and J7723 was withdrawn from use on 11 May 1928. Features of the Guan lived on, however, as the same design of high altitude wing and high-set tailplane were used in the Gambet naval fighter for Japan.

The first Gloster Guan, J7722, was fitted with a geared Napier Lion engine and a Gloster-made Hele-Shaw Beacham variable-pitch propeller. Designed as a high-altitude Gamecock development, it had a significantly increased upper wing span. (Author's collection)

Close-up of the previous photograph showing the supercharger plumbing, oil cooler (below the gun trough) and radiator. Although guns are not fitted there is a bomb carrier just aft of the radiator. (Author's collection)

The second Guan, J7723, with direct drive Napier Lion and radiator shutters open. (Author's collection)

Guan details

Single-seat high-altitude interceptor. Two prototypes: J7722 and J7723. Third prototype (J7724) cancelled. 3 Gloucestershire Guan ordered on Contract No 570353/25 dated January 1925 to Specification 17/24.

Construction: steel fuselage and wooden wings, fabric covered.

Engine:
J7722: geared Napier Lion IV of 450 hp (336 kW) with external exhaust-driven turbo-supercharger below propeller shaft, with 9 ft 8 in (2.95 m) dia. wooden or variable-pitch metal propeller.
J7723: direct-drive Napier Lion VI of 525 hp (392 kW) with supercharger above propeller shaft, with fixed-pitch metal propeller.
J7724: Lioness. Cancelled.

Armament: gun troughs on fuselage sides, twin .303 (0.77 mm) Vickers guns not fitted.

Dimensions: Span 31 ft 10 in (9.7 m) (upper wing). Length 22 ft (6.7 m). Height 10 ft 2 in (3.1 m). Wing area 298 sq ft (27.7 sq m).

Performance and weights:
J7722: top speed 155 mph (249 km/h) at 16,000 ft (4877 m). Climb to 20,000 ft (6096 m) 12 min. Service ceiling 31,000 ft (9449 m). All-up weight loaded 3,660 lb (1660 kg), tare 2,859 lb (1297 kg).
J7723: top speed 175 mph (282 km/h) at 15,000 ft (4572 m). Climb to 20,000 ft (6096 m) 12.5 min. Service ceiling 31,000 ft (9449 m). All-up weight loaded 3,803 lb (1725 kg), tare 2,972 lb (1348 kg).

Gambet and Nakajima A1N

By 1926 Gloster's Sparrowhawk fighters, the Bentley BR2-engined Nighthawks supplied to Japan in 1922, were entering their fifth year of service and in April the Imperial Japanese Navy put out a specification to Nakajima, Aichi and Mitsubishi to replace them and the Mitsubishi Type 10 (1MF4). Nakajima, with licence production in mind and appreciating Gloster's experience with the Nightjar naval fighter (another BR2-engined Nighthawk variant, designed for the Fleet Air Arm) made enquiries about a navalised version of the Gamecock. Glosters responded with the Gambet, developed for shipboard operation.

In July 1927 Nakajima negotiated the purchase of the prototype, powered by a 420 hp (313 kW) Jupiter VI with wooden propeller, as a pattern aircraft, together with the manufacturing rights. It was first flown by Howard Saint at Brockworth on 12 December 1927 and shipped to Japan early the following year.

Gloster had initiated the Gambet design as a navalised Gamecock before the Japanese specification was issued, possibly as a Fairey Flycatcher I replacement for the Fleet Air Arm. Company advertising listed the Gambet's special features as "*Easy accessibility to engine and all essential parts, ideal gun position, robust construction, special Gloster biplane combination, tanks easily detachable and gravity feed, excellent manoeuvrability*". Details of the Gambet's performance were submitted to the Air Ministry, together with the offer of sending the machine to Martlesham for testing. The company claimed an improvement of 15 mph (24 km/h) over existing carrier fighters, but the ministry did not take up the offer.

Gloster's Gambet naval fighter, the pattern aircraft for the A1N-1 built by Nakajima for the Imperial Japanese Navy. (Author's collection)

The unmarked Gambet photographed at Brockworth, clearly showing the full-height windscreen which Folland first used on the Nighthawk and the high-mounted tailplane. The stencil markings give only the component numbers (a 5-digit number beginning G.5/153) and the doping scheme code T4S (Titanine doping scheme no. 4, sprayed). (Author's collection)

This front view of the Gambet at Brockworth shows the difference in span between upper and lower wings. (Download from news.webshots.com)

GLOSTER "GAMBET"

TYPE	Single Seater High-Speed Deck Landing Scout.
ENGINE	420 h.p. Bristol Jupiter Aircooled Radial, Series VI.
DIMENSIONS	Total Surface ... 284 sq. ft. ... 26·385m². Span ... 31' 10" Top, 26' 0" Bottom 9·702m.—7·925m. Chord ... 5' 6¼" ... 5' 2¼" ... 1·688m.—1·587m. Gap ... 5' 0" ... ... 1·524m. Wing Section Special High Lift Biplane Construction.
TANKAGE	Petrol: Two 36-gallon tanks mounted in Top Planes. Gravity feed. Total capacity ... ... 72 gallons ... 327 litres Oil ... ... 7 ... 31 „
PERFORMANCE	Speed at 5,000 ft. (1,524m.) ... 152 m.p.h. ... 245 kms. „ 10,000 ft. (3,050m.) ... 145 m.p.h. ... 233 „ „ 15,000 ft. (4,570m.) ... 138 m.p.h. ... 222 „ Climb ... ... 3 mins. to 5,000 ft. (1,524m.) „ ... ... 7 „ to 10,000 ft. (3,050m.) „ ... ... 11 „ to 15,000 ft. (4,570m.) Ceiling ... ... 23,000 ft. ... 7,000m. Landing Speed ... 49 m.p.h. ... 79 kms. Duration: 3½ hours at 15,000 ft. (4,570m.) with full load.
WEIGHTS	Total loaded weight of machine, 3,075 lbs. ... 1,397 kg. Load per sq. ft. ... 10·83 lbs./sq. ft. ... 52·954 kg./m². Load per H.P. ... 7·32 lbs./h.p. ... 3·28 kg./C.V.
ARMAMENT	Two Vickers Guns at sides of fuselage, firing through propeller. Provision for bomb racks to carry 4—20 lb. (9 kg.) bombs.
SPECIAL FEATURE	Easy accessibility to Engine and all essential parts, Ideal Gun Position, Robust Construction, Special Gloster Biplane Combination, Tanks easily detachable and Gravity Feed, Excellent Manœuvrability.

THE GLOSTER AIRCRAFT Co., Ltd.,
SUNNINGEND WORKS, CHELTENHAM.

London Office : 5, GRAFTON STREET, BOND STREET, W.1

Right   No. 4.

Details of the Gambet were published in this Gloster advertisement of 1928. The length is not given and is still not known for certain. (Author's collection)

An image from the internet of an Imperial Japanese Navy Nakajima A1N-2. (Website not traced)

A young Kenji Ozaki poses beside his Nakajima A1N-1. He survived the war after flying a reconnaissance plane as an intelligence officer - he was sent home with malaria, making him the only survivor of his squadron. The only things he possessed at the war's end were this photo and his suicide dagger. Ozaki eventually became a senior local government officer near Tokyo and refused to speak of his experiences. (via John Adams)

Structure was wood and similar to the Gamecock in major respects (while the Gamecock was the RAF's last wooden fighter, the Gambet was the last wooden fighter to be produced by Gloster). The wings and tail were similar in format to the Guan, the top wing having no centre section and being joined on the centre line like the Gamecock, but with a span greater than the Gamecock at 31 ft 10 in (9.7 m) and with long parallel chord ailerons in line with the trailing edge. The overhang of the top wing was braced with streamline wires

J-AAMB was a navy-surplus Nakajima A1N-1 used as a mailplane in the late 1930s. It has acquired an exhaust collector ring, an enclosed cockpit and a lengthened fin but has lost its oleo undercarriage. (Via Jack Meaden)

attached in a similar way to the vee struts of the later Gamecock. The fuel tankage was increased over that of the Gamecock by 22 gallons (100 l) to 72 (327 l), the fuselage was lengthened and the engine had stub exhausts and a pointed nose like the civil Gamecock G-EBNT and the Finnish Gamecock II. The tail unit had the Gamecock-type rounded tailplane and square-tipped elevators, but mounted at the top of the fuselage like the Goldfinch, Gorcock and Guan. It had a Gamecock-type rudder but an almost straight tapered fin. Arrester claws were fitted on the undercarriage spreader bar.

Produced by Nakajima with a 520 hp (388 kW) Nakajima-built Jupiter VI engine, under the design leadership of Takao Yoshida, it was accepted in April 1929 after competing against Japanese designs and designated the Navy Type 3 Carrier Fighter A1N-1. Fifty were built with flotation gear fitted in a shallow streamlined bulge under the fuselage between the undercarriage legs. The first aircraft to enter service joined the aircraft carriers *Akagi*, *Hosho* and *Kaga*, replacing the Mitsubishi Type 10. Later, in 1933, they also served on the carrier *Ryujo*.

In 1930 a development was introduced, the A1N-2 with the 450 hp (336 kW) Nakajima Kotobuki engine installed with a dish-shaped front cover with radial cooling slots and a metal propeller. About a hundred were built between 1930 and 1932.

A1Ns were used operationally against the Chinese in the Shanghai Incident of January to March 1932. On 22 February A1Ns flown by PO3c Toshio Kuro-iwa and Lieutenant Nokiji Ikuta shot down Robert Short, a US mercenary flying a Chinese Boeing P-12E. In 1935 the type was withdrawn from service.

Changes made in service included the flotation gear being removed for operations from shore stations and navigation lights being fitted for night flying. The late production A1N-2 had very slim circular section front undercarriage legs with no hint of shock absorbers, a reminder that in 1931 a Gloster designer, George Dowty, had designed an internally-sprung wheel for fighter undercarriage of which details were published in the technical press. This attracted the attention of Kawasaki in Japan who indicated to Dowty that they were prepared to order six. Gloster were invited to produce these but lost their opportunity by too high a quote and Dowty left Gloster to form his own small company, later to become the multi-company Dowty Group. Kawasaki tested these on their KDA-5 Type 92 biplane fighter in 1932 and this led to the Japanese producing their own version, which may explain the plain legs on the A1N-2.

After Gloster provided the prototype Gambet, some liaison continued during licence production and it is possible that this included development advice, as at least one A1N-2, perhaps an experimental model, had a modified top wing with rounded tips similar to those on the Gamecock II.

While stub exhausts seemed to be accepted happily by the Japanese and Finns on their open cockpit fighters, an A1N-1 registered J-AAMB, which was converted in Japan for civil use as a mailplane with an enclosed cockpit, had a frontal collector ring and two underwing exhaust pipes in a similar fashion to the RAF Gamecock I. This suggests that stub exhausts had allowed some effects of fumes to be felt in the cockpit.

No more Gloster fighters were to appear with the tail underfin inherited from Folland's first world war SE5 or with the Folland/Preston HLB wing configuration, but quite a few of the Grebe-Gamecock line continued in operation well into the 1930s in Britain, as did the Gambet variants in the Far East, while the Finnish version of the Gamecock served into the 1940s.

Gambet / Nakajima A1N-1 and A1N-2 details

Single-seat naval fighter. One pattern aircraft built by Gloster, no serial number. Approx. 50 built by Nakajima as Type A1N-1 and approx. 100 as Type A1N-2.

Construction:
wooden fuselage and wings, fabric covered.

Engine:
Gambet: Bristol Jupiter VI of 420 hp (313 kW) with Watts 9 ft (2.74 m) dia. wooden propeller.
A1N1: Nakajima Jupiter VI of 520 hp (388 kW) with 9 ft 2 in (2.79 m) wooden propeller.
A1N2: Nakajima Kotobuki 2 of 450 hp (336 kW).

Armament:
Gambet: two .303 (7.7 mm) Vickers guns; provision for bomb racks to carry 4 x 20 lb (9 kg) bombs.
A1N-1 and A1N-2: two 7.7 mm machine guns; two 30 kg bombs under wings.

Dimensions:
Span: upper wing 31 ft 10 in (9.7 m), lower wing 26 ft 0 in (7.92 m).
Length is disputed: it is not quoted in any original Gloster material; Derek James states 21 ft 3.5 in, Mikesh and Abe state 21 ft 3.75 in, Jack Meaden states 21 ft 4 in (6.49 to 6.5 m); recent research by John Adams suggests 20 ft 3 in (6.17 m).
Height: Gambet and A1N-1 10 ft 8 in (3.25 m). A1N-2 10 ft 10 in (3.3 m). Wing area 284 sq ft (26.38 sq m).

Performance and weights:
Gambet: top speed 152 mph (245 km/h) at 5,000 ft (1524 m). Climb to 10,000 ft (3048 m) 7 min. Service ceiling 23,200 ft (7071 m). All-up weight 3,075 lb (1395 kg). Tare weight 2,010 lb (912 kg).
A1N-1: top speed 148 mph (238 km/h) at 5,000 ft (1524 m). Climb to 10,000 ft (3048 m) 7.05 min. Service ceiling 24,410 ft (7440 m). All-up weight 3,197 lb (1450 kg). Tare weight 2,094 lb (950 kg).
A1N-2: top speed 150 mph (241 km/h) at 5,000 ft (1524 m). Climb to 10,000 ft (3048 m) 6.3 min. Service ceiling 25,520 ft (7778 m). All-up weight 3,031 lb (1375 kg). Tare weight 1,944 lb (882 kg).

Gorcock J7502 in its final configuration.

Guan J7723.

Goldfinch J7940.

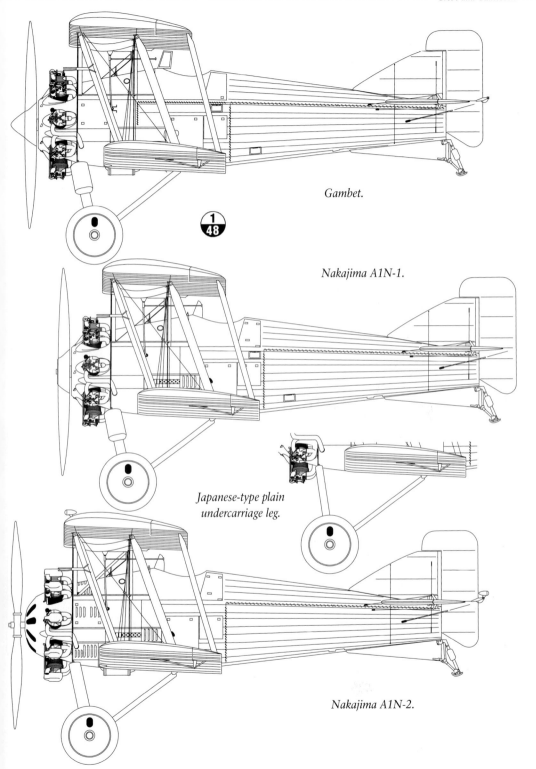

Gambet.

Nakajima A1N-1.

Japanese-type plain undercarriage leg.

Nakajima A1N-2.

Henry Folland

Henry Folland was one of Britain's most distinguished aircraft designers and one of very few to design famous fighters of both World Wars: the SE5A and the Gladiator. He was responsible for three other RAF front-line fighters, the Grebe, Gamecock and Gauntlet, and three more for overseas air forces: the Nighthawk for Greece and the Sparrowhawk and Gambet for Japan.

Folland also designed a remarkable series of racers, from the Bamel - three times winner of the Aerial Derby - to the beautiful Gloster VI seaplane which failed to take part in the 1929 Schneider Trophy contest but captured, albeit briefly, the world absolute speed record. There were many other experimental types, almost all military, including a WW1 triplane bomber, a troop carrier so large that trenches had to be dug for the wheels to get it out of Gloster's hangar and a high-performance monoplane fighter which came close to be being adopted to serve alongside the Spitfire and Hurricane.

Henry Phillip Folland was born in Cambridge in 1889, the son of a stonemason. Between 1905 and 1912 he was in Coventry, first as an engineering apprentice with the Lanchester Motor Co and then as an engineering designer with the Daimler Motor Co. He married Muriel Bayliss Warner and moved to Farnborough in 1912, where he worked under Geoffrey de Havilland on the FE2, RE1 and SE2. His first accredited design was a souped-up SE2 development, the SE4, which set an unofficial speed record of 135 mph (217 km/h) in 1914 and was criticised as being "too fast".

Henry Phillip Folland OBE FRAeS FIAeS FRSA (1889-1954) was one of the outstanding aircraft designers of his day. Here at the Royal Aircraft Factory in 1914, the cap-wearing Folland, aged only 25, stands with his first accredited design, the SE4, on the right of the picture. It was easily the fastest aeroplane in the world, clocking up 135 mph (217 km/h) powered by a 14-cylinder two-row Gnome rotary of 160 hp (119 kW). (Walwin Collection)

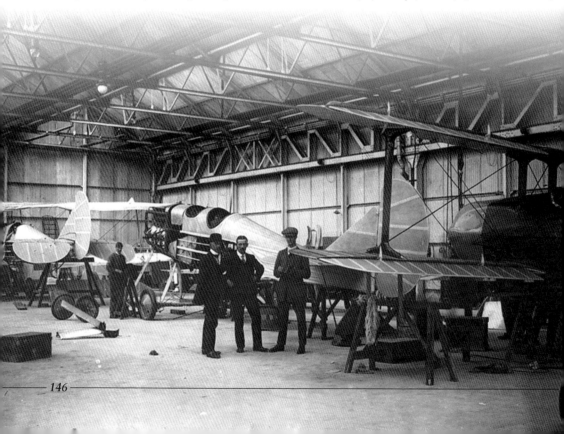

Folland and SJ Waters produced the hopelessly inadequate FE4 twin-engine, two-seat pusher biplane in 1916, but Folland now met HE (Henry) Preston, who became his loyal assistant and stressman for nearly 40 years and shares the credit for most of his subsequent designs. Next off the drawing board was Folland's first major success, the SE5 fighter, soon developed into the SE5A and proving to be one of the best fighters of any air force in the First World War.

When the Royal Aircraft Factory design team was dispersed in 1917 Folland, Preston and several other factory staff joined the Nieuport & General Aircraft Co in Cricklewood. His BN1 and Nighthawk fighters and Goshawk racer are described in the main text. His London triplane bomber was the only other "British Nieuport" design to be built but he also schemed single- and two-seater light aircraft, biplane and triplane passenger aircraft and a passenger flying boat.

Joining the Gloucestershire Aircraft Company first as a consultant, then as chief engineer and designer, Folland went on to design the Grebe and Gamecock series of aircraft with the High Lift Biplane (HLB) wing configuration which he patented with Preston. They also patented the distinctive rubber-cum-oleo undercarriage used by these Gloster types.

Folland was essentially a conservative designer, advancing by careful development and refinement. When he tried something more daring, such as the inverted tripod undercarriage of the SE4, it was not always successful. Indeed, the HLB wing form combined with lack of conventional upper wing centre section may have worked well enough on the Grebe but was prone to so much flutter as power, speed and wingspan increased that it was not capable of further development. Folland put strength and safety first with his next front-line RAF fighter, the Gauntlet, a two-bay biplane with conventional wing sections.

Folland's Gauntlet and Gladiator are well known and have been written about ably and comprehensively by Alex Crawford in other books in this series. The next major turning point in Folland's career came in 1934, the year of the Gladiator's first flight, when Gloster was taken over by the Hawker Aircraft Co. Hawker's chief designer, Sydney Camm, was in the ascendant and Folland's days at Gloster were numbered. His reputation was such that he was able to obtain financial backing to buy the British Marine Aviation Company at Hamble in 1937, soon changing its name to Folland Aircraft Ltd. The company was extremely successful as a sub-contractor but no more of Folland's own designs were built. The Folland 43/37 engine test bed was designed by Frank Radcliffe, who also went to Hamble from Gloster, and no other Folland aircraft would fly until Edward Petter's Midge light fighter in August 1954. Folland died early the following month, aged 64.

Gloster test pilot and chief designer: Larry Carter (left) and Henry Folland. (via Derek James)

Test pilots

Larry Carter

Larry Carter replaced "Jimmy" James as Gloster's test pilot in April 1923, arriving as the HLB programme was getting under way. Between then and June 1925 he was responsible for all the in-house testing and development of the Grebe, Gamecock and Gorcock.

Lawrence Lauder Carter was born near Devizes on 17 February 1898. After school at Christ's Hospital he trained as an engineer in the Parsons turbine works in Newcastle-on-Tyne. He joined up in 1915 and served with 29 Squadron RFC in France, downing five enemy aircraft. Wounded in the last encounter - shot through the sciatic nerve with an explosive bullet - he was posted back to Britain and became an instructor at Shrewsbury.

"*Wondering what to do next*" after the war, as he put it, he embarked on an epic flight from London to Stockholm in June 1920, together with Norwegian aviation pioneer and adventurer Major Tryggve Gran MC, in a war-surplus Armstrong Whitworth FK8. (Gran had a remarkable career. He was ski instructor to Scott's expedition to the South Pole and it was he who discovered the bodies of Scott and his companions in 1910. Four years later he was the first man to fly the North Sea, crossing from Scotland to Norway in just over four hours in a Blériot monoplane, only a year after Blériot himself flew the English Channel. He assumed a Canadian identity to join the RFC and claimed to have shot down Herman Göring in September 1917. He died in 1980 aged 90.)

Larry Carter was Gloster's second chief test pilot, succeeding "Jimmy" James. This portrait from the Cheltenham Chronicle and Graphic was reproduced in the company house journal's obituary of Carter in 1926. (Via Jet Age Museum)

Carter became a demonstrator for the Bristol Aeroplane Company in August 1921, showing off several Bristol types in Spain, before joining Handley Page Continental Air Services as an airline pilot. He made more than a hundred flights between London and Paris, carrying 644 passengers in the course of 260 flying hours. On 3 May 1922, as he was taking off from Le Bourget with seven passengers, the undercarriage fell off but he carried on and landed at Croydon "*with very little damage to his machine and without the slightest shock to his passengers. In fact, they were not aware that anything was wrong until they were acquainted with the fact after descending from the machine*" (those were the days!). Henry Folland wrote in 1926: "*On two occasions I was privileged to occupy the spare pilot's seat. ... I little thought at the time that a few months later we should be working side by side in the interests of aeronautical development.*"

Carter won the Aerial Derby Handicap in 1922, flying the Lucifer-engined Bristol M1 monoplane G-EAVP. He resigned as an airline pilot at the end of March 1923 to join the Gloucestershire Aircraft Company, going

Larry Carter immediately after winning the 1923 Aerial Derby in Gloster I G-EAXZ, an improved version of the Bamel. Lack of centre section and inverted vee struts foreshadow the arrangement of the Grebe and Gamecock; tailplane, fin and rudder are the same as the Grebe; and the engine cowling, forward-leaning front vee struts and Lamblin radiator are similar to those of the first Gorcock, J7501. (Author's collection)

The Gloster II in readiness at RAF Cranwell before the high-speed flight which ended with Carter's crash landing. (David Pearce)

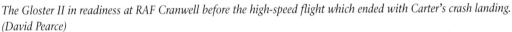

The wreckage of the Gloster II after Carter landed at some 200 mph (about 320 km/h). The metal propeller bent on impact and acted as a skid, saving Carter's life, but he was badly injured. (David Pearce)

on to win both the Aerial Derby Race and Handicap that year in the Gloster I at an average speed of 192.4 mph (310 km/h).

His career ended with the crash of the Gloster II. This was described in the company's house magazine The Gloster as *"the firm's reply to America's bid for air supremacy. Built purely for research work on racing aircraft, she marked a big step forward in British design. Her test flights were attendant with risks as her top speed was over 250 miles an hour (more than 400 km/h)."* While flying this machine at Cranwell on 10 June 1925 he made a forced landing at about 200 mph (about 320 km/h), his injuries including a fractured skull. He recovered slowly, although he did not fly again, but he later developed meningitis and died in Cheltenham on 27 September 1926, aged 28.

Maurice Piercey

Maurice W Piercey was a freelance pilot who stepped in as a temporary Gloster test pilot in 1926-27 after Carter's accident. He tested and demonstrated Grebes and Gamecocks - in April 1926 Flight published a great photo set of one of his Gamecock demonstrations - and he gave an impressive display in the Gorcock at the 1927 RAF Display at Hendon.

At Carter's funeral he flew a Gamecock over the burial service in salute. Gloster chief inspector Basil Fielding recalls flying with Piercey in a two-seater Grebe and beating up a garden party in Upton St Leonards, on the far side of Brockworth airfield. When Brockworth was open to the public as one of the stages of the 1926 King's Cup air race, Piercey demonstrated both Grebe and Gamecock, as well as Folland's ultralight Gannet. This had been an unsuccessful contender in the 1922 Lympne light aeroplane trials but had been re-engined with a Blackburne [sic] Tomtit of a mere 26 hp (19.4 kW). One visitor claimed that Piercey flew in and out of one of the hangars in the Gannet, although the company house journal The Gloster stated *"we are inclined to discredit this report"*.

Maurice Piercey, in breeches and flying helmet, poses in front of an early Gamecock together with the Brockworth airfield team. (Via Jet Age Museum)

Maurice W Piercey had been a Flight Sergeant in the Royal Flying Corps, promoted to Lieutenant in March 1918, then becoming a Flying Officer in the new Royal Air Force. He was awarded the Air Force Cross in June 1919 and left the service in September. He spent the next few years as a racing and competition pilot, flying an ANEC in the Lympne light aeroplane trials of 1923 and gaining first prize in the Beardmore Wee Bee 1 in the trials the following year. 1925 saw him demonstrating the Dutch-registered Pander light monoplane H-NACO at Croydon.

Out of a job in 1927 after Saint's appointment, Piercey is next heard of competing in July's King's Cup Air Race in an ANEC II. The last published reference to him is in September that year when he accompanied Captain RH McIntosh, an Imperial Airways pilot, in the Jupiter-engined Fokker F.VIIA monoplane Princess Xenia from Bristol to Baldonnel, Dublin. A fortnight later McIntosh failed to fly non-stop from Dublin to New York, but it is not clear that Piercey was with him on the transatlantic attempt.

Howard Saint

Gloster waited until after Carter's death to appoint a new chief test pilot, which they did in January 1927. This was Flying Officer Howard Saint, who had been awarded the Distinguished Service Cross as a Royal Naval Air Service fighter pilot on Sopwith Triplanes and Camels. He flew the Grebe with VP propeller, the Gamecock and its derivatives and later the Goral, the SS18 and 19 and Gauntlet - "*the finest aircraft the company ever pro-*

duced". Other types including the AS31 survey biplane, the lumbering Gloster TC33 troop carrier and the even more lumbering DH72 trimotor biplane bomber, which had been completed at Brockworth. He left the company when it was taken over by Hawker in 1934, being replaced by PEG "Jerry" Sayer.

Howard John Thomas Saint was born in Ruabon, near Wrexham, in 1893. He joined the RNAS in 1915, trained as a pilot the following year and was one of 15 officers under aviation pioneer Godfrey Paine who started the flying school which became RAF Cranwell. Posted to 5 Wing as a bomber pilot, he took part in the raid on the Brussels Zeppelin sheds. He was posted to 10 Naval Squadron in 1917 and after scoring seven victories transferred to Martlesham, where he commanded B Flight. It was there that he flew DH9 C6053 on a record endurance flight, the first of more than seven hours, in February 1918 with Lt Thompson RNVR as observer.

He resigned in 1919 and as senior pilot to Air Transport and Travel was holder of the

Royal Naval Air Service ace Howard Saint DSC was Britain's first commercial airline pilot, then Gloster's fourth chief test pilot between 1927 and 1934. He was noted for his ability to recover from a Gamecock in a spin. (Via Derek James)

first British commercial pilot's licence. On May 1, the day on which civil aviation was first permitted after the war, he was flying to Bournemouth with some newspapers and with DM Greig, general manager of ATT as passenger on the first registered civil machine, DH9 G-EAAA, when he crashed on the hills behind Portsmouth. He fractured his jaw and sustained minor injuries. From 1922 he was a test pilot at RAE Farnborough until he joined Gloster.

After Gloster Saint spent a year with Parnall at Yate, then retired from active flying in 1936. He was manager of Doncaster Airport between 1936 and 1938, then went to Shoreham and a year later to Heston. He worked for the Ministry of Aircraft Production during the war and afterwards with the Ministry of Works (as assistant director) and the Ministry of Supply. His last job was back at Farnborough, where he was contracts officer in the Space Department.

Saint finally retired in 1965 aged 72. He had flown more than 250 aircraft types and amassed more than 14,000 flying hours. He died in Cheltenham in 1976 aged 83.

Captain Saint and Lieutenant Thompson RNVR after their DH9 was the first aircraft to remain in the air for more than seven hours in August 1917. After 3 hours 30 minutes at 15,000 feet (4572 m) they had to descend to 3,500 feet (1067 m) to unfreeze the radiator, before returning to 15,000 feet until their fuel was almost exhausted. (Via Jet Age Museum)

Howard Saint poses for the Flight cameraman with the Gamecock II and his dog Buster. (Flight photo via Jet Age Museum)

Appendices

Serials and Registrations

Civil

GROUSE I & II	G-EAYN Modified Mars III (Sparrowhawk II) with experimental HLB wings
GREBE	G-EBHA Fourth Grebe prototype, retained for company use
	Company demonstrator, Jupiter trials, VP propeller trials
GAMECOCK	G-EBNT Company demonstrator
	G-EBOE (Orion engine). Not completed as G-EBOE, completed as J9248
	G-ADIN Former Gamecock "III" J8047 sold to JW Tomkins
NAKAJIMA A1N1	J-AAMB Former Imperial Japanese Navy A1N1

ROYAL AIR FORCE and other UK military

GREBE	J6969 - J6971	3 prototypes
	J7283 - J7294	12 Grebe II
	J7357 - J7402	46 Grebe II
	J7406 - J7417	12 Grebe II
	J7519 - J7538	20 Grebe IIIDC
	J7568 - J7603	36 Grebe II
	J7784 - J7786	3 Grebe II
GAMECOCK	J7497	1st prototype
	J7756 - J7757	2nd and 3rd prototypes
	J7891 - J7920	Gamecock I
	J7959	Gamecock I
	J8033 - J8047	Gamecock I
	J8069 - J8095	Gamecock I
	J8405 - J8422	Gamecock I
	J8804	Gamecock II
	J9248	Gamecock (Orion). Originally G-EBOE , not completed as such
GOLDFINCH	J7940	
GORCOCK I/II	J7501 - J7503	
GUAN	J7722 - J7724	

SWEDISH ARMY AIR SERVICE

GROUSE II	62	Previously Sparrowhawk II / Grouse I / Grouse II G-EAYN
		Sold to Sweden 9 December 1925

NEW ZEALAND PERMANENT AIR FORCE

GREBE II	NZ501	Previously J7381 (29 Squadron RAF)
	NZ502	Previously J7394 (29 Squadron RAF)
	NZ503	Previously J7400 (R33 airship trials, then 25 Squadron RAF), converted to dual control for NZPAF
	A-5	Formerly NZ-501
	A-6	Formerly NZ-502

FINLAND

GAMECOCK	GA-38	Gloster-built Gamecock II pattern aircraft
	GA-43	Gloster-built Gamecock II pattern aircraft (long fuselage)
KUKKO	GA-44 - GA-47	4 Finnish-built Gamecock II with lengthened fuselage and modified tail
	GA-48 - GA-58	11 Finnish-built second production batch

JAPAN

GAMBET	(no ID)	1 Gloster-built pattern aircraft
NAKAJIMA A1N1	?	50 Nakajima-built. Serials included 208, 224, 252
NAKAJIMA A1N2	?	100 Nakajima-built. Serials included 203, 212, 221, 236, 255

Gloucestershire or Gloster?

The Gloster Aircraft Company was originally the Gloucestershire Aircraft Company, formed in Cheltenham 1917, so contemporary reports refer to the Gloucestershire Grebe and Gamecock. In 1923 a development of the Mars I "Bamel" racer was called the Gloster I and on 11 November 1926 the name of the company itself was changed to Gloster, to simplify spelling and pronunciation, especially for overseas customers. Nowadays it is usual to use the name Gloster to refer to the company and its aircraft whatever the date.

Brockworth or Hucclecote?

In the early years production took place in Cheltenham. After WW1 the Aircraft Acceptance Park sheds and aerodrome at Brockworth, near Gloucester, were rented for hangarage and flying. Production was transferred to Brockworth in stages during the 1920s, except for the Schneider Trophy racers, which were still made in Cheltenham. Eventually the company offices were also relocated to Brockworth Aerodrome. The parish boundary with neighbouring Hucclecote runs through the site and in 1930 Gloster officially adopted Hucclecote as its postal address, apparently because this ensured two postal deliveries a day. It was normal, though, to continue to refer to the airfield itself as Brockworth except in official company documents.

Model kits

GREBE
Aeroclub
K033: 1/72 Grebe II. Injection + white metal. Decals for 25, 29 and 32 Squadrons RAF.
K410: 1/48 Grebe II. Vacform + white metal. Decals for 32 Squadron RAF.
Merlin Models
No. 9: 1/72 Grebe II and IIIDC. Injection. Decals for 56 Squadron RAF and for NZPAF NZ-501.

GAMECOCK
Aeroclub
K034: 1/72 Gamecock I. Injection + white metal. Decals for 17, 23, 32 and 43 Squadrons RAF.

K406: 1/48 Gamecock I. Vacform + white metal. Decals for 23 Squadron RAF.
Broplan
MS-108: 1/72 Gamecock II. Injection. Decals for GA-43, 45, 46, 50. 51, 52, 55.
MS-112: 1/72 Gamecock II. As above but with skis.
Czech Master Resin
CMR-32: 1/72. Gamecock I. Resin. Upgraded 2009. No decals.
Montex
RMA3202. 1/32 Gamecock I. Resin. Paint masks for 23 and 32 Squadrons RAF.
Galdecal
GAL72008: 1/72 Finnish Collection. Decal set includes Gamecock II GA-43 and GA-45, 1929.

There was an injection-moulded Gamecock by Pegasus (Kit No. 007, without decals but with drawing showing 3 Squadron markings) and another by Veeday (kit no. 012 with decals for J8035 of 43 Squadron - also issued as double kit 012/013 with Fairey Flycatcher). There was reputedly also a resin Gamecock kit by Private Venture C.

NIGHTHAWK AND NIGHTJAR
Blue Rider
BR106: 1/72 Nieuport Nighthawk (Gloucestershire Mars VI Nighthawk with Armstrong-Siddeley Jaguar engine). Vacform kit with white metal and photoetched brass details. Decals for H8544 and HR8544 with 1 Squadron RAF, Iraq 1923; D84 with Greek Army Air Force, 1923-38.
BR105: 1/72 Nieuport Nightjar (Gloucestershire Mars X Nightjar with Bentley BR2 engine). Vacform kit with white metal and photoetched brass details. Decals for H8537, 203 Squadron RAF; "2", 203 Squadron RAF, Kilill Bahr, Gallipoli 1923; and H8539, RAE Farnborough 1922.

GAMBET / NAKAJIMA A1NI / A1N2
Choroszy Modelbud
A15 : 1/72 Nakajima A1N1. Production Gloster Gambet. Resin. Decals for numbers 212 and 224.
A16: 1/72 Nakajima A1N2. Gambet development. Resin. Includes number 212.

References

Books
Beedle, J: 43 Squadron: The History of the Fighting Cocks 1916-66. Beaumont, London, 1966.
Bridgman, Leonard, and Oliver Stewart: The Clouds Remember. Arms and Armour Press, London, 1972 (first pub. 1936).
Duval, GR: RAF Fighters 1918-37. Bradford Barton, Truro, 1975.
Goulding, James: Interceptor. Ian Allan, London, 1986.
Grey, CG, (ed): Jane's All the World's Aircraft 1924. Sampson Low, London, 1924.
--- Jane's All the World's Aircraft 1925. Sampson Low, London, 1925.
James, Derek N: Gloster Aircraft since 1917. 2nd ed, Putnam, London 1987.
--- Fighter Master Folland and the Gladiators. Tempus, Stroud, 2007.
Jefford, CG: RAF Squadrons. Airlife, Shrewsbury, 1988.
Lumsden, Alec SC: British Piston Aero-Engines and Their Aircraft. Airlife, Marlborough 2003 (first pub. 1994).
--- and Owen Thetford: On Silver Wings: RAF Biplane Fighters Between the Wars. Osprey, London, 1993.
Mason, Francis K: The Gloster Gamecock (Profile 33) . Profile Publications, Windsor, 1971.

--- The British Fighter since 1912. Putnam, London, 1992.

Mason, Tim: British Flight Testing: Martlesham Heath 1920-1939. Putnam, London, 1993.

Meekcoms, KJ and EB Morgan: The British Aircraft Specifications File. Air-Britain, Tonbridge, 1994.

Mikesh, Robert C, and Shorzoe Abe: Japanese Aircraft 1910-1941. Putnam, London, 1990.

Mowthorpe, Ces: Battlebags: British Airships of the First World War. Sutton, Stroud, 1998 (first pub. 1995).

Munson, Kenneth: Fighters Between the Wars 1919-39. Blandford, Poole, 1970, reprinted 1977.

Ord-Hume, AWJG: British Fighting Biplanes. GMS Enterprises, Peterborough, 2005.

Penrose, Harald: British Aviation: The Adventuring Years 1920-29. Putnam, London, 1973.

--- British Aviation: Widening Horizons 1930-34. HMSO, London, 1979.

Rawlings, John DR: Fighter Squadrons of the RAF and their Aircraft. Macdonald, London, 1969.

Rimell, Raymond L: RAF Between the Wars. Arms and Armour Press, London, 1985.

Sinnott, Colin: The RAF and Aircraft Design 1923-1939: Air Staff Operational Requirements. Frank Cass, London, 2001.

Thompson, Dennis, and Ray Sturtivant: Royal Air Force Aircraft J1-J9999. Air Britain, Tonbridge, 1987.

Wheeler, Allen: Flying Between the Wars. GT Foulis, Henley-on-Thames, 1972.

Magazine articles

Aeroplane Monthly
> May 1974: James, Derek N: "A Country Gamecock".
> September 1994: Brett, Maurice: "A Question of Plumage" [Grebe squadron markings].
> December 1998: --- "A Brace of Gamecock?"

Air Enthusiast
> April-July 1983 (No. 21): Green, William, and Gordon Swanborough: "The Era-Ending Gamecock".

Air Pictorial
> August 1963: JM Bruce: Nieuport Nighthawk Part 1.
> September 1963: --- Part 2.
> September 1965: FA Yeoman: The Gloster Grebe.
> October 1968: T: Mason: The Nighthawk Family (Martlesham Miscellany - 3).

Air Review
> January 1947: JWR Taylor.

Airfix Magazine
> July, August & September 1973: Robertson, Bruce: "Fighting Colours 1914-1937", parts 13-15.

Flight
> 9 February 1922: Gloucestershire Goods Type Commercial Aeroplane.
> 2 July 1925: Hallo, Mosquitoes!
> 1 October 1925: The RAF in Army Manoeuvres.
> 12 November 1925: Grouse feature.
> 19 November 1925: Grebe feature.
> 28 October 1926: R33 as Aircraft Carrier.
> 2 December 1926: R33 Makes Further Test.
> 7 July 1927: Grebes in RAF Display.
> 17 November 1927: Flg Off C Mackenzie-Richards killed.
> 16 August 1928: Grebe for New Zealand.
> 4 October 1928: Gloster Goldfinch.
> 11 July 1929: Two-seater Grebe wins King's Cup (Gloster advertisement).
> 3 July 1931: and Day's Gamecock display at Hendon.
> 20 June 1946: Grebe carburettor icing.

12 September 1952: AVM RL Ragg CB CBE AFC.
27 May 1955: Gloster 40th anniversary special feature.
17 May 1962: Long Look Back by John Yoxall
18 March 1971: Grebe carburettor de-icing.

"The Gloster"
(Gloster Aircraft Company house magazine): various issues

Scale Aircraft Modelling
March 1983: Mike Keep: Royal Air Force Colours 1920-39.
--- Ian Huntley: Finnish Colours.

Archives

Air Publications
AP1124: Gloucester Grebe Aeroplane Schedule of Spare Parts. 2nd ed. March 1926.
AP1139. Jaguar Series IV Aero Engine. 2nd ed. May 1928.
AP1168: The Grebe Aeroplane. November 1927 (supersedes AP1168, April 1925).
AP1190: Gloster Gamecock Aeroplane Schedule of Spare Parts. 2nd ed. March 1927.
AP1196: Gamecock (Jupiter VI Engine) Rigging Notes. 1st ed. November 1925.
AP1278: Jupiter VI Aero Engine. 1st ed. March 1927.
AP1299: Gamecock Aeroplane Jupiter VI Engine. 1st ed. December 1927.

National Archives
AIR20/100. Gamecock fighter aircraft: tests.

Jet Age Museum archives
Burroughes, Hugh: The Gloster Story (RAeS lecture, Gloucester January 1967).
Carter, John H: History of Gloster Aircraft Co Ltd. Unpublished in-house company history (no date).
Fielding, Basil: unpublished memoirs of Gloster chief inspector.
Gloster Aircraft Company:
--- List of Contracts Executed.
--- Notes and photographs of individual aircraft types.
--- Press cuttings July 1928- July 1929; January - July 1930; January -May 1931.
--- 1/48 and 1/72 scale three-view drawings.
--- Company brochure "Series No. 2: Gloster Machines in RAF Displays" (The Aeroplane supplement 4 July 1928).
--- Company brochure "Series No. 5: Gloster Hele-Shaw Beacham Variable Pitch Airscrew".
--- Company brochure "Series No. 6: Gloster Metal Construction" (The Aeroplane supplement 24 October 1928).
Jones, Roff T: Grebe and Gamecock archive material; design notes and drawings for Gamecock replica.
Meaden, Jack, and John Whitaker: 50 Years of Gloster Aircraft (typescript draft of uncompleted book).

Misc

RNZAF First Day Cover commemorating the 60th anniversary of the first test flight of Gloster Grebe NZ501 of the NZPAF Wigram on 2 March 1928, posted 2 March 1988, with history of NZ Grebes on card insert.

Websites

New Zealand Military Aircraft Serial Numbers: Gloster Grebe: www.adf-serials.com/nz-serials/nz502.shtml
www.avrosys.nu/aircraft/ Skol/indexskol.htm, 18 July 2005: Grouse in Swedish service
Håkan Gustavsson's "Håkan's Aviation Page" at http://surfcity.kund.dalnet.se/index.html

Gamecock reproduction

No Gamecock survives, but a reproduction Gamecock I is nearing completion in Jet Age Museum's workshop at the Tithe Barn Centre in Brockworth, not far from the site of the former Gloster Aircraft Company's factory-airfield. No mere look-alike, it is as accurate as the museum's volunteers have been able to make it.

The project was initiated by Jet Age chairman John Lewer, then keeper of aircraft for Gloucestershire Aviation Collection, the registered charity which trades as Jet Age Museum. A representative collection would have to include at least one of Gloster's between-the-wars fighters. The Gamecock was chosen because it was of largely wooden construction and an engine was available.

The design team was led by the late Roff T Jones, a former Gloster senior designer and engineer who had joined the company in 1937. He brought together a team of veteran designers and draughtsmen and they held their inaugural meeting on 27 February 1993 at HH Martyn Co's Sunningend factory in Cheltenham, where the original Gamecock had been built. The company provided the team with a drawing office for the next few years.

There are no complete survivors of any of Gloster's High Lift Biplane series. Rear fuselage sections of two Finnish-built Gamecocks survive in museums in Finland, but apart from a handful of components that is all.

Examining castings for the Gamecock undercarriage oleo produced by Stroud Technical College, July 1994. (L to R) Don Tombs (Gamecock designer-draughtsman), Dave Blackwell (Stroud), Roger Gribble (Stroud), Roff T Jones (Gamecock project chief designer), Mike Portlock (Stroud). (E Currier LRPS)

The reproduction is a remarkable achievement, because hardly any original Gamecock drawings have survived either. The few original drawings available were for the Finnish version, widely differing from the RAF version and with all captions in Finnish. Working from these and known dimensions for the RAF Gamecock I, the chance discovery of an original spares manual and a limited range of other sources, Roff and his team produced a priceless set of many hundred construction drawings to the highest possible standard.

The drawings were passed to the late Barry Denton, who led the construction team. Volunteers got to work in workshops and sheds around the county and in August 1998 at Staverton a basic fuselage and tail unit, with engine, propeller and undercarriage, was dedicated by Ida Whitaker, daughter of Gloster company founder AW Martyn, on her 100th birthday. The Gamecock then had to go into store when the Jet Age hangar at Staverton was redeveloped, but it was moved to the Tithe Barn Centre in 2007, when the workshop there became available, and work resumed.

A few compromises have been made - the rigging wires are circular rather than streamline section due to cost, and plywood is used instead of asbestos for the firewall - but otherwise it is pretty much spot on. The engine is on loan from the RAF Museum and was reconditioned by Rolls-Royce Heritage Trust. The propeller is original, as are one interplane strut and two inter-aileron struts, one of them restored after it had been sharpened as a fence post.

The Gamecock reproduction is being finished as J7904 of 43 Squadron as flown by the squadron commander, complete with black and white chequers on the rear fuselage spine.

Gamecock project construction team manager Barry Denton poses by his shed with the newly-completed fin, rudder and tailskid unit in the early 1990s. (E Currier LRPS)

Gamecock project dedication by Ida Whitaker, daughter of Gloster Aircraft Company founder AW Martyn, at Staverton on her 100th birthday in August 1998. (Author's collection)

The tailplane incidence lever on the port side of the cockpit. (Author's collection)

Detail of the fin and rudder with wireless aerial attachment. (Author's collection)

The aluminium map case hinged open on the mahogany veneered plywood instrument panel. (Author's collection)

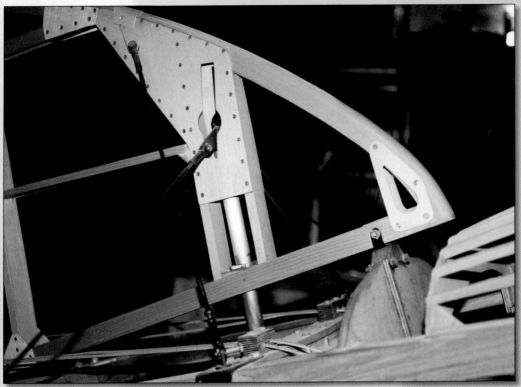

Detail of the fin and rudder with wireless aerial attachment. (Author's collection)

The aluminium map case hinged open on the mahogany veneered plywood instrument panel. (Author's collection)

Gloster's patent oleo undercarriage employed rubber shock absorbers in a streamlined casing. (Author's collection)

Fuselage priming and painting in progress #1. (Author's collection)

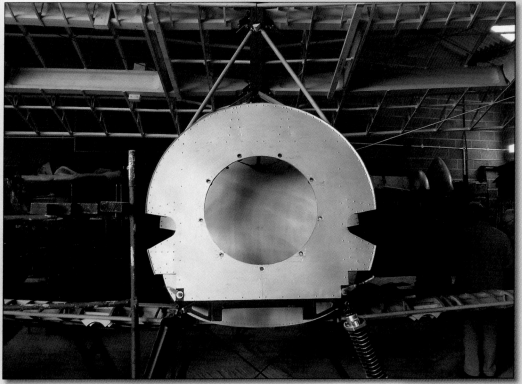

Near-circular fuselage cross-section behind engine, with cut-outs for machine gun troughs. (Author's collection)

Fuselage priming and painting in progress #1. (Author's collection)

Arrangement of centre section struts. (Author's collection)

Fuselage priming and painting in progress #2. (Author's collection)

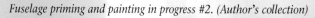

Detail of fuel tank in port upper wing. (Author's collection)

Metal fuselage panels being fitted. (Author's collection)

Gun mounting detail showing associated steel tube fuselage bracing. (Author's collection)

Rear fuselage and tail covered and painted #1. (Author's collection)

Tail showing bracing and rudder control wires. (Author's collection)

Rear fuselage and tail covered and painted #2. (Author's collection)

Steel tube centre section struts with wooden fairings on the diagonals. (Author's collection)

Rear fuselage and tail covered and painted #3. (Author's collection)

Jet Age Museum's Gamecock reproduction in March 2011 as it neared completion. Some underside panels were still to be fitted. Original components include the Jupiter engine, on loan from the Royal Air Force Museum, the propeller, spoked wheels, underwing generator, the port interplane strut and the two inter-aileron struts. The starboard side will remain uncovered to show the structure and workmanship. (Author's photo)

The rear fuselage of Finnish-built Gamecock Mk II GA-58 (production number 15) in Suomen Ilmailumuseo, the Finnish Aviation Museum. It was delivered on 15 May 1930 and crashed on 10 March 1940, killing its pilot. Total hours logged were 688 hours 35 minutes. (Reino Myllymäki: http://upload.wikimedia.org)

Colour profiles

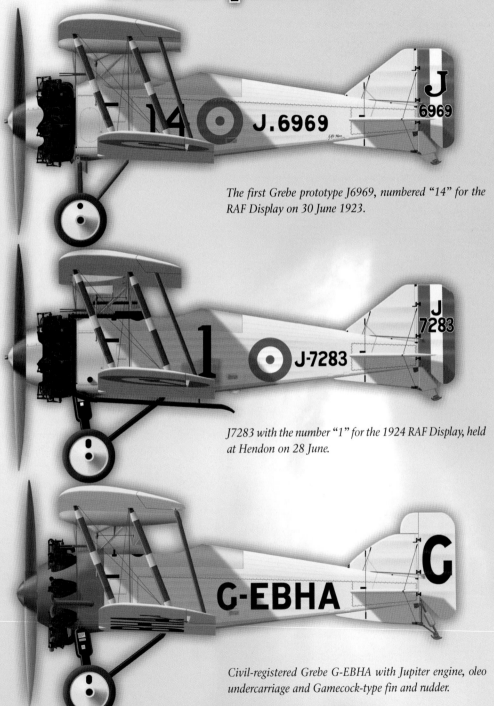

The first Grebe prototype J6969, numbered "14" for the RAF Display on 30 June 1923.

J7283 with the number "1" for the 1924 RAF Display, held at Hendon on 28 June.

Civil-registered Grebe G-EBHA with Jupiter engine, oleo undercarriage and Gamecock-type fin and rudder.

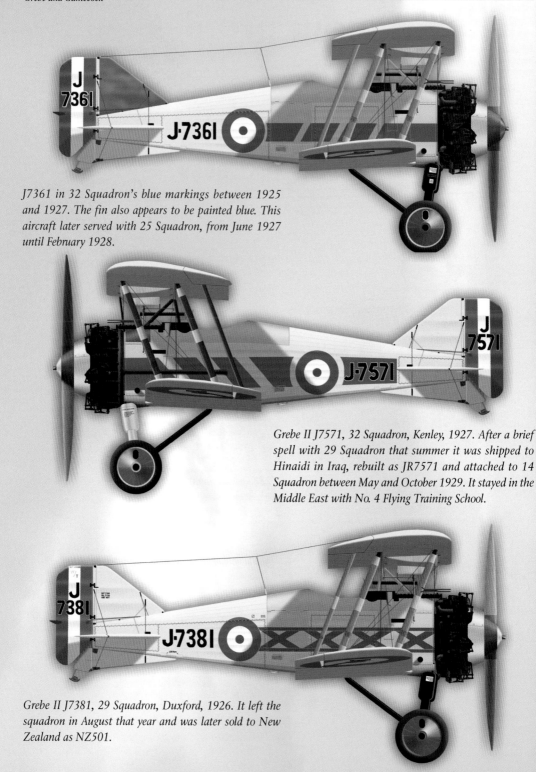

J7361 in 32 Squadron's blue markings between 1925 and 1927. The fin also appears to be painted blue. This aircraft later served with 25 Squadron, from June 1927 until February 1928.

Grebe II J7571, 32 Squadron, Kenley, 1927. After a brief spell with 29 Squadron that summer it was shipped to Hinaidi in Iraq, rebuilt as JR7571 and attached to 14 Squadron between May and October 1929. It stayed in the Middle East with No. 4 Flying Training School.

Grebe II J7381, 29 Squadron, Duxford, 1926. It left the squadron in August that year and was later sold to New Zealand as NZ501.

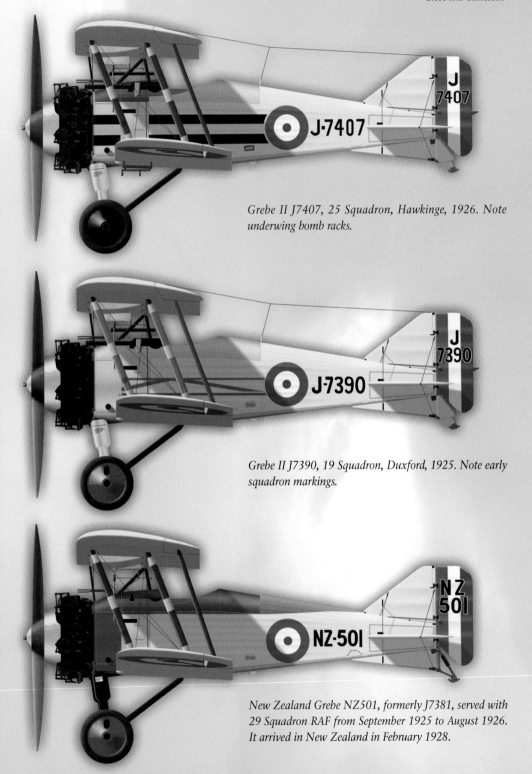

Grebe II J7407, 25 Squadron, Hawkinge, 1926. Note
underwing bomb racks.

Grebe II J7390, 19 Squadron, Duxford, 1925. Note early
squadron markings.

New Zealand Grebe NZ501, formerly J7381, served with
29 Squadron RAF from September 1925 to August 1926.
It arrived in New Zealand in February 1928.

Grebe II J7400 was used for the first air-launch trial with the airship R33 in 1926.

Grebe II J7363, 25 Squadron, S/L AH Peck DSO, Hawkinge, 1926. The a/c wears ID bands on the rear fuselage and the lower wings as well as an X on the starboard cockpit coaming.

Top view of J7363.

Bottom view of J7363.

Starboard view of J7363. Note bomb racks under fuselage.

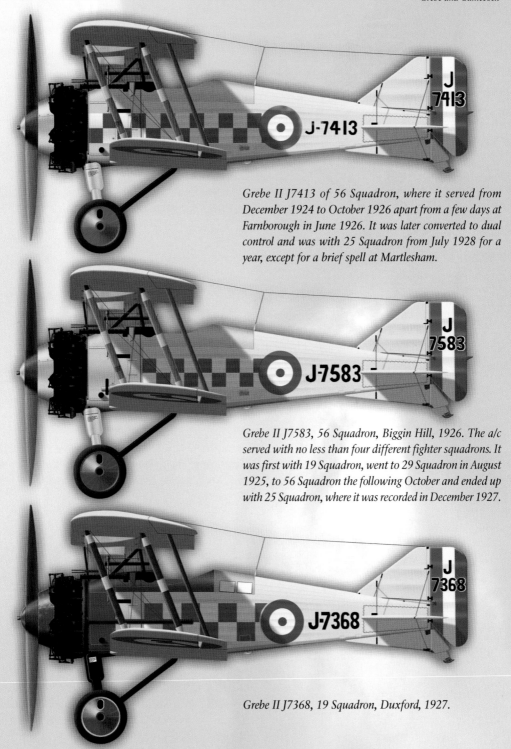

Grebe II J7413 of 56 Squadron, where it served from December 1924 to October 1926 apart from a few days at Farnborough in June 1926. It was later converted to dual control and was with 25 Squadron from July 1928 for a year, except for a brief spell at Martlesham.

Grebe II J7583, 56 Squadron, Biggin Hill, 1926. The a/c served with no less than four different fighter squadrons. It was first with 19 Squadron, went to 29 Squadron in August 1925, to 56 Squadron the following October and ended up with 25 Squadron, where it was recorded in December 1927.

Grebe II J7368, 19 Squadron, Duxford, 1927.

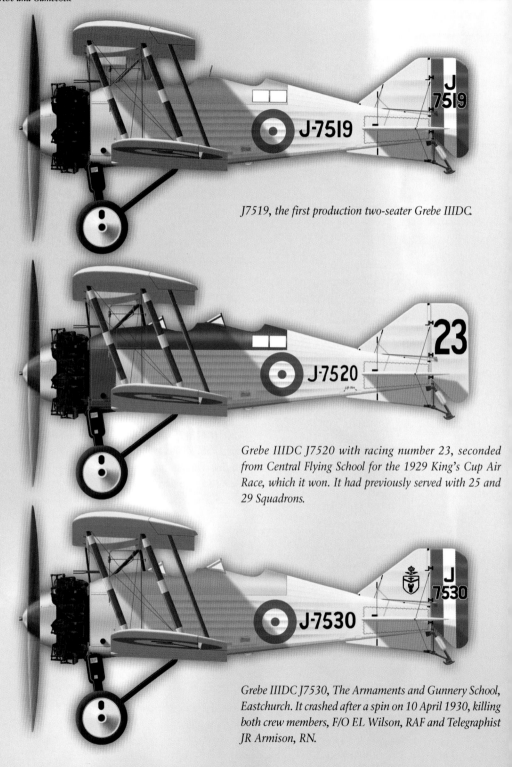

J7519, the first production two-seater Grebe IIIDC.

Grebe IIIDC J7520 with racing number 23, seconded from Central Flying School for the 1929 King's Cup Air Race, which it won. It had previously served with 25 and 29 Squadrons.

Grebe IIIDC J7530, The Armaments and Gunnery School, Eastchurch. It crashed after a spin on 10 April 1930, killing both crew members, F/O EL Wilson, RAF and Telegraphist JR Armison, RN.

Two-seater NZ503, ex-J7400, rebuilt for New Zealand. It was delivered in 1928.

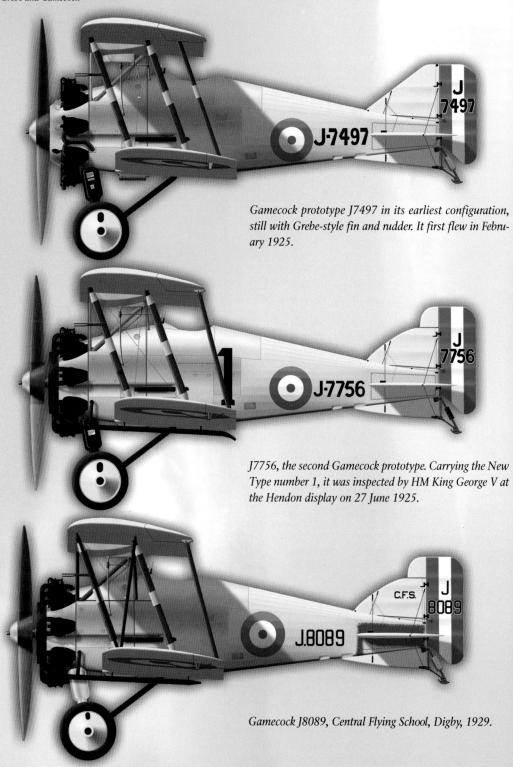

Gamecock prototype J7497 in its earliest configuration, still with Grebe-style fin and rudder. It first flew in February 1925.

J7756, the second Gamecock prototype. Carrying the New Type number 1, it was inspected by HM King George V at the Hendon display on 27 June 1925.

Gamecock J8089, Central Flying School, Digby, 1929.

Gloster's civil unarmed demonstrator Gamecock G-EBNT.

G-EBNT, top view

G-EBNT, bottom view

G-EBNT, starboard view

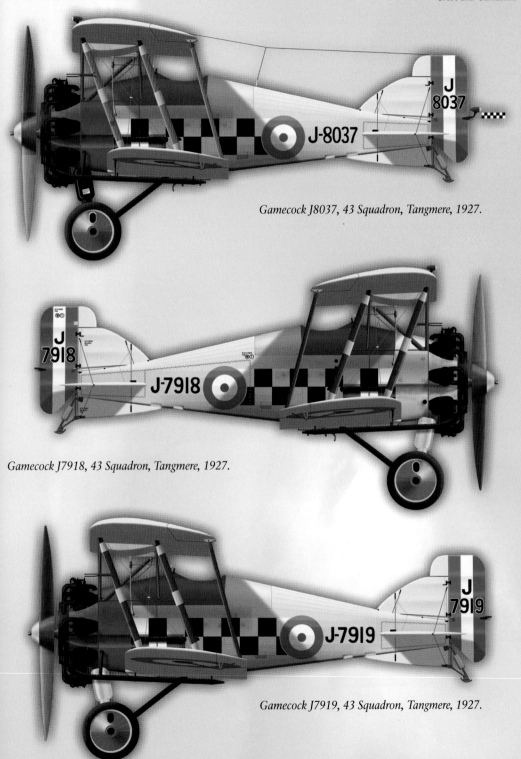

Gamecock J8037, 43 Squadron, Tangmere, 1927.

Gamecock J7918, 43 Squadron, Tangmere, 1927.

Gamecock J7919, 43 Squadron, Tangmere, 1927.

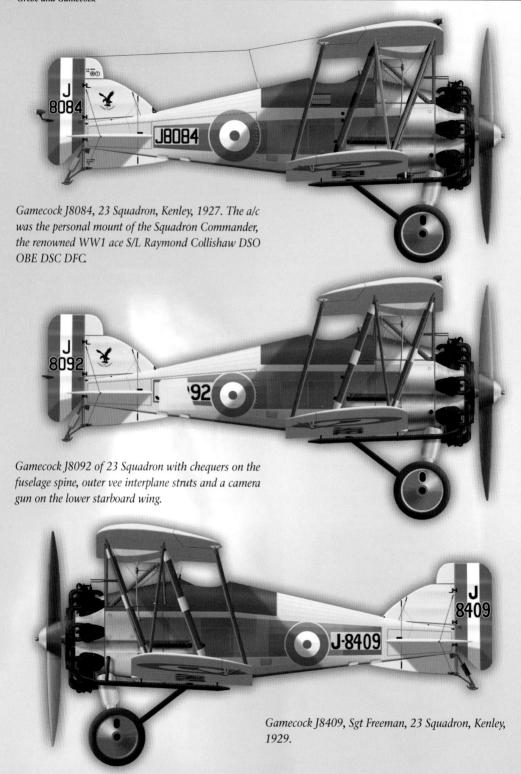

Gamecock J8084, 23 Squadron, Kenley, 1927. The a/c was the personal mount of the Squadron Commander, the renowned WW1 ace S/L Raymond Collishaw DSO OBE DSC DFC.

Gamecock J8092 of 23 Squadron with chequers on the fuselage spine, outer vee interplane struts and a camera gun on the lower starboard wing.

Gamecock J8409, Sgt Freeman, 23 Squadron, Kenley, 1929.

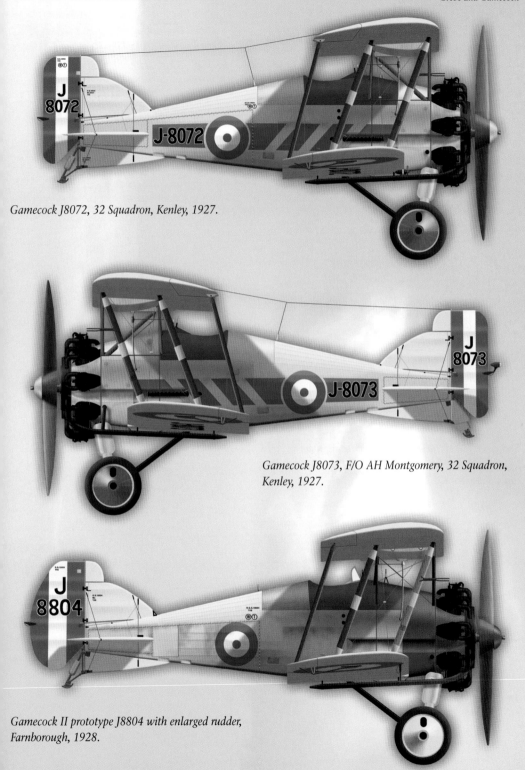

Gamecock J8072, 32 Squadron, Kenley, 1927.

Gamecock J8073, F/O AH Montgomery, 32 Squadron, Kenley, 1927.

Gamecock II prototype J8804 with enlarged rudder, Farnborough, 1928.

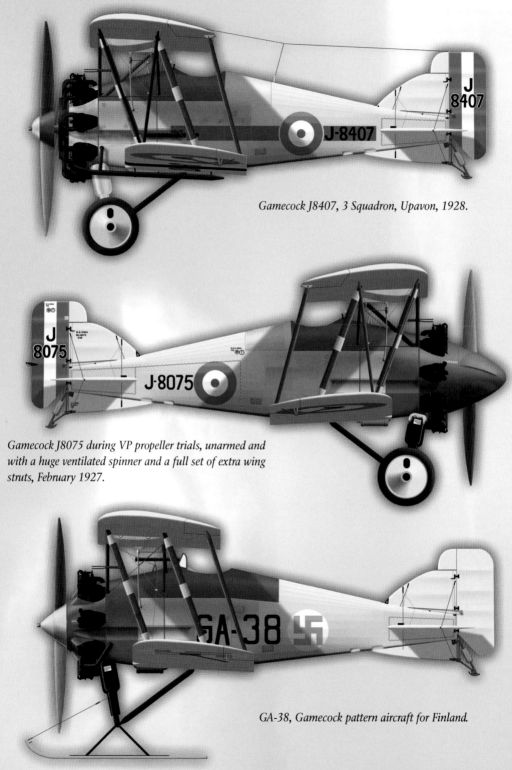

Gamecock J8407, 3 Squadron, Upavon, 1928.

Gamecock J8075 during VP propeller trials, unarmed and with a huge ventilated spinner and a full set of extra wing struts, February 1927.

GA-38, Gamecock pattern aircraft for Finland.

Gamecock J7908, 43 Squadron, Tangmere, 1927.

Top view of J7908.

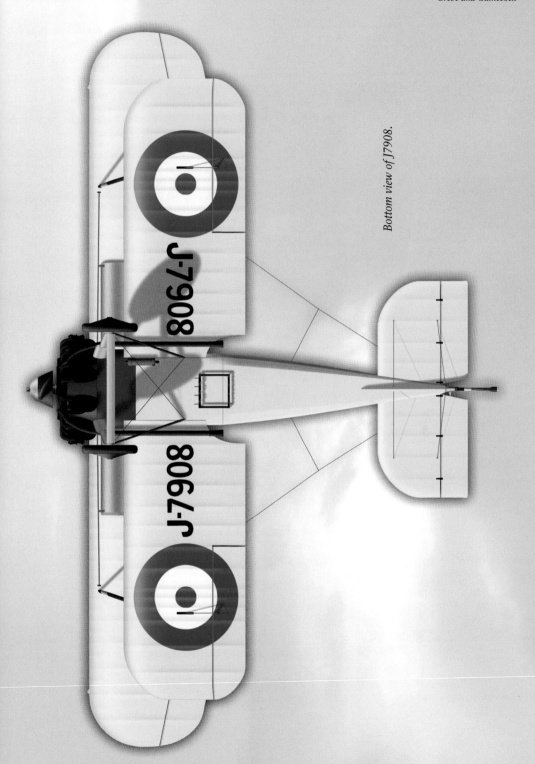

Bottom view of J7908.

Starboard view of J7908.

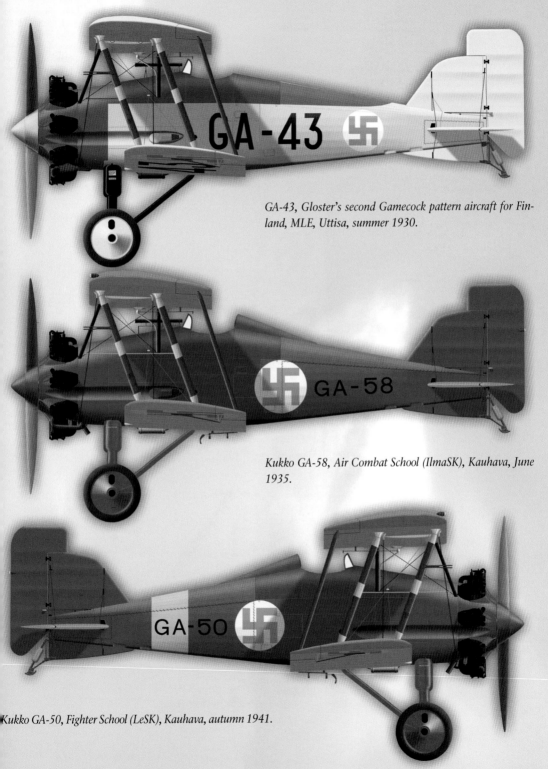

GA-43, Gloster's second Gamecock pattern aircraft for Finland, MLE, Uttisa, summer 1930.

Kukko GA-58, Air Combat School (IlmaSK), Kauhava, June 1935.

Kukko GA-50, Fighter School (LeSK), Kauhava, autumn 1941.

Kukko GA-52, MLE, Utissa, winter 1931.

Kukko GA-52, top view.

Kukko GA-52, bottom view.

Kukko GA-52, starboard view.

Gamecock "III" prototype J8047, Brockworth, June 1928.

Goldfinch J7940, Martlesham, May 1927.

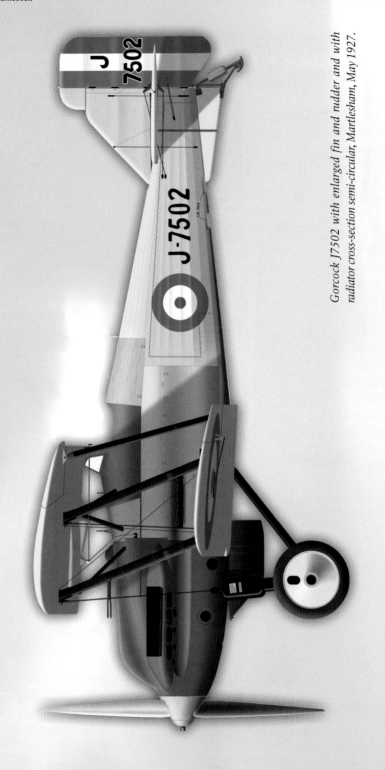

Gorcock J7502 with enlarged fin and rudder and with radiator cross-section semi-circular, Martlesham, May 1927.

The second Guan, J7723, with direct drive Napier Lion, Farnborough, April 1927.

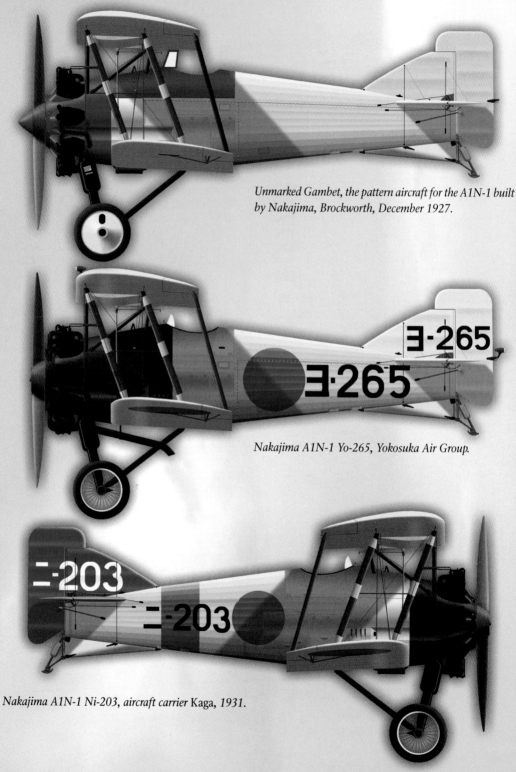

Unmarked Gambet, the pattern aircraft for the A1N-1 built by Nakajima, Brockworth, December 1927.

Nakajima A1N-1 Yo-265, Yokosuka Air Group.

Nakajima A1N-1 Ni-203, aircraft carrier Kaga, 1931.

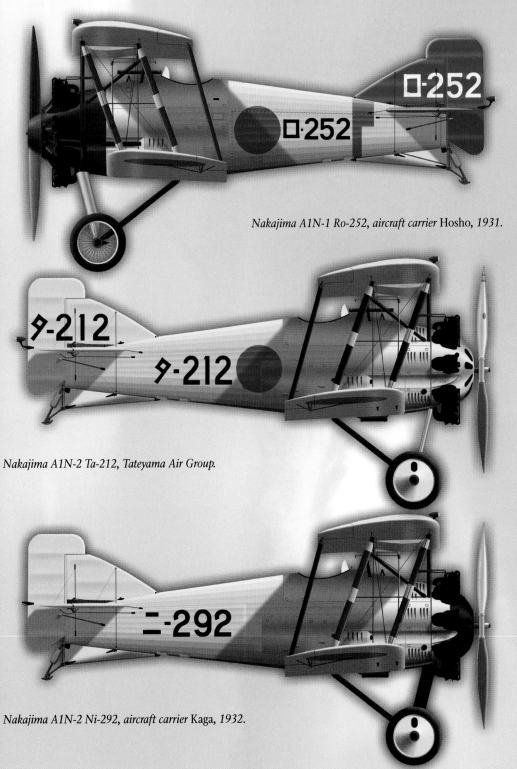

Nakajima A1N-1 Ro-252, aircraft carrier Hosho, 1931.

Nakajima A1N-2 Ta-212, Tateyama Air Group.

Nakajima A1N-2 Ni-292, aircraft carrier Kaga, 1932.

Nakajima A1N-2 Ni-236, aircraft carrier Kaga, 1932.